Yellow Pages of Learning Resources

**Resources Directory
Area Code 800**

National Association of Elementary
School Principals
1801 North Moore Street
Arlington, Virginia 22209

The MIT Press
Cambridge, Massachusetts,
and London, England

Educational Facilities Laboratories, Inc.
477 Madison Avenue
New York, New York 10022

Group for Environmental Education Inc.
1214 Arch Street
Philadelphia, Pennsylvania 19107

edited by
Richard Saul Wurman

written by
George Borowsky
Peter Cotton
Nancy Donovan
Natasha Stonorov
Rae Zielin
Joan Chait
Sunny Decker

printed and bound by Semline, Inc.
in the United States of America

Second printing, August 1972

Library of Congress catalog card number: 72-3398
ISBN: 0-262-23061-5 (hardcover)
ISBN: 0-262-73032-4 (paperback)

Contents

**Yellow Pages
of Learning
Resources**

WITHDRAWN

Editor's Note

This booklet is only a handshake with a city. We hope that it will serve as a welcome mat to the endless possibilities for learning all around you. We hope it will reduce your anxieties about using your community as the schoolhouse it really is, and we hope, in turn, you will add greatly to our brief listings.

Somehow, even as modest an undertaking as this requires a great deal of empathy and help. This has been heaped on this project by the many people interviewed, by the authors, by the staff of the MIT Press, and through the generous support of Educational Facilities Laboratories, Inc. The book was conceived in response to "The Invisible City" International Design Conference in Aspen with the help of George Borowsky, Nancy Donovan, Natasha Stonorov, and Rae Zielin. I would like to thank this core group and extend a particular note of thanks to Peter Cotton, who compiled the appendix. I also thank Kat Marin for permission to reprint in the appendix certain items that appeared in an article by Jane Lichtman in the newsletter *New Schools Exchange.*

Richard Saul Wurman

Introduction

Why a *Yellow Pages of Learning Resources*?
The city is education—and the architecture of education rarely has much to do with the building of schools. The city is a schoolhouse, and its ground floor is both bulletin board and library. The graffiti of the city are its window displays announcing events; they should reveal its people to themselves, tell about what they're doing and why and where they're doing it. Everything we do—if described, made clear, and made observable—is education: the "Show and Tell," the city itself.

This book is concerned with the potential of the city as a place for learning.

Education has been thought of as taking place mainly within the confines of the classroom, and school buildings have been regarded as the citadels of knowledge. However, the most extensive facility imaginable for learning is our urban environment. It is a classroom without walls, an open university for people of all ages offering a boundless curriculum with unlimited expertise. If we can make our urban environment comprehensible and observable, we will have created classrooms with endless windows on the world.

What Is the *Yellow Pages of Learning Resources*?
This book is an invitation to discover the city as a learning resource.

The purpose of the *Yellow Pages* is to turn people on to learning in the city and to assist them in taking advantage of the wealth of available learning opportunities. There are three basic parts to this invitation. First, the *Yellow Pages* provides a selection of typical firsthand learning resources that can be found in almost any city. These examples and the others they suggest serve to make vivid the richness of learning potential readily at our disposal. The examples of typical learning resources included in the *Yellow Pages* are intended to indicate the depth and breadth of available learning possibilities. There are thousands of others that might have been considered had there been time and room enough. You will find those that most interest you. The key is to start realizing the learning potential in the people, places, and processes we encounter every day.

Second, the *Yellow Pages* outlines the avenues to follow in order to make these resources accessible. This is the "where" and "how" of converting people, places, and processes into sources of learning. The aim of this book is to encourage readers, through the examples provided, to extend their own entrepreneurial abilities to locate and utilize additional resources for learning. The extent of accessible learning resources is limited only by the reader's imagination and sensitivity to his environment.

We assume that schools are the places for education, and we believe we know when we are being taught. As a result, most of us are apathetic when it comes to self-learning. We have television, light shows, teaching machines, cinerama, and a whole host of simulation techniques—a vast technology for making the artificial seem real. But in the glamor of our sophisticated informational and educational technologies we often fail to appreciate the reality in our everyday lives; we no longer place a premium on experiential learning. Reality is frequently too obvious, and we are rapidly becoming jaded. Too often, we no longer look carefully, listen intently, or yield to our innate sense of wonder.

Yet the city is everywhere around us, and it is rife with invaluable learning resources. Even more than classrooms and teachers, the most valuable learning resources in the city are the people, places, and processes that we encounter every day. But in order to realize the vast learning potential of these resources, we must learn to learn from them.

We should learn to differentiate between products and performance. We must learn to use the city, to explore. We must learn not to overlook the obvious. We must learn to hear when we listen, to see when we look, to ask questions, and to realize that good questions are better than brilliant answers. We must learn to demand from our city that it fulfill its potential as a learning resource. Each of us should recognize his role as the developer of an invitation to learning.

We should be concerned about real experiences and encourage the development of new learning situations that are independent of traditional books and learning products, which focus on student experiences in classrooms and school buildings. We should be interested in the identification and the subsequent communication of the elements that make up the man-made environment. We should understand the need to develop the skills and abilities to communicate information about the environment both verbally and nonverbally. We should create in a student the confidence that will enable him to develop the criteria that might be used in the evaluation or creation of his own environments. And we should remember that we are all students. We should encourage a sense of ownership of the city and define the extent of the public environment. We should see the "environment issue," not simply as the causes and effects of air and water pollution, but in broader terms: the understanding of the total physical environment, both public and private.

This book is full of questions. These are provided in order to suggest how rich the learning resources can be and to cultivate the learning process by planting the seeds of inquiry. Questions, rather than answers, are the beginning of learning, but too often we find it difficult to pose good questions.

Learning from People

In a very real sense the city is its people. Everybody can be a teacher. From a bank president to the guy next door—including the mailman, Uncle Charlie, a carpenter, a shopkeeper, and everyone else—everybody knows things, has been places, and has answers. The city is full of people to learn from—all we have to do is start asking questions and demonstrate enough interest to deserve the answers.

Then, too, each of us can be both learner and teacher. Once we have unleashed our own curiosity, we can easily appreciate other people's quest to know and understand. We need, therefore, to be open and willing to share our knowledge and understanding with each other. To other people, we are the other people.

Learning at Places

Classrooms are not the only places for learning. There are many other spaces that could be used for people to get together and learn in. While we search around for spaces in which to meet, learn, play, rest, or think, thousands of spaces are going unused in every city. Our cities are very inefficient because we do not use effectively the spaces we have. Ironically, we are wasting valuable space by using it for only small parts of the day; at the same time we complain of the need for more classrooms. Office conference rooms, public auditoriums, waiting rooms, movie theaters, churches, building lobbies—just to name a few—are always there, even when they are not being used. How could we begin to take advantage of the city's underutilized spaces?

As well as being spaces for meeting and learning in, many places are themselves learning resources. Very often things can best be learned by experiencing them firsthand. Why read about how a port operates when there is one a short bus ride away? Why read a book about how steel is made if there is a steel plant nearby? Does it make sense to study about crime and police protection services without ever visiting a real police station?

Any place where special things happen or that possesses unique characteristics (and all places do when you think seriously about them) can be a rich learning resource. That it is not fancy or designed for learning makes it especially valuable. Street corners, hospitals (in which one can learn about bookkeeping and food preparation, as well as about medicine), stores, gas stations, airports, electricity generating plants, banks, and insurance companies are all good places for learning, and experiential learning is the most interesting and the most fun.

Learning about Processes

We usually tend to think of things only as products instead of considering the roles they play in larger processes. Telephones are small parts of the process of communication, automobiles are parts of transportation, and doctors are parts of health care. When we enlarge our thinking to seek an understanding of whole processes, we consider cause-and-effect relationships, change over time, interrelationships among parts, and total concepts. Just think of all the processes required daily to make a city possible!

Good questions lead us eventually to want to know how a process works from beginning to end. When we mail a letter, how does it find its way to its destination? By what means do our cities grow and change? Where does the food we eat come from, and what happens to it along the way? The daily processes affecting each of our lives are constant invitations to learning, once we cease taking them for granted.

Who Can Use the *Yellow Pages of Learning Resources*? Just about everyone—children, high-school students, parents, and teachers. This book is written so that children can understand it and use it themselves. However, several of the learning resources outlined here are especially suited to group learning experiences— guided tours, field trips, and demonstrations of particular skills. It is hoped that parents and teachers, as well as children, will read this book and find in it suggestions for learning experiences that they can both utilize themselves and share with the younger learners who look to them for guidance.

The *Yellow Pages of Learning Resources* can also be used by people in every city and town. No matter how small your town is, it is rich in learning resources to be tapped. The following chart provides a sample list of resources in many different areas—from a large city of almost two million people right down to a small town of just over two thousand!

	Philadelphia, Pennsylvania	Baltimore, Maryland	Cincinnati, Ohio	Albuquerque, New Mexico	Columbus, Ohio	Altoona, Pennsylvania	Wausau, Wisconsin	Tulare, California	Aspen, Colorado
Population	1,948,609	905,759	452,524	243,751	154,168	62,900	32,806	13,824	2,404
Advertising agencies (indoor and outdoor)	330	195	134	38	9	8	8	1	5
Architects	445	175	166	84	15	9	6	n.a.	15
Auto registrations	613,902	269,193	150,841	142,869	100,427	33,000	19,138	9,164	n.a.
Banks	22 main 339 branches	savings 5 commercial 7 savings and loan 295	comm. and sav. 116 sav. and loan 246	comm. 6 branches 29 sav. and loan 7	savings 9 sav. and loan 5	comm. 2 sav. and loan 5	comm. 6 sav. and loan 2	4	3
Department stores	95 main 140 branches	59	53	23	28	15	10	6	3
Doctors (M.D.s only)	4,000	2,193	1,130	347	139	101	65	19	12
Electric meters	539,204	584,308	427,722	98,669	57,621	20,888	28,657	n.a.	n.a.
Gas meters	539,261	421,669	312,059	81,826	48,645	20,580	12,303	n.a.	n.a.
Hospitals (general)	40	29	28 (in area)	8	3	3	4	4	1
Junk yards and dealers	85	52	21	7	6	5	2	n.a.	n.a.
Lawyers	5,420	2,458	1,470	432	146	50	53	10	19
Libraries (all kinds)	183 (plus branches)	66 (24 br. free lib.)	66 (35 br. of pub. lib.)	13 (6 br. of pub. lib.)	4	4	5	1	1
Newspapers (daily)	3	2	2	2	2	1	1	1	0
Newspapers, magazines, and trade publications	285	99	69	17	6	5	1	1	4
Photographic processing plants	350	205	170	100	33	17	6	6	7
Printing (printers and establishments)	545	356	241	62	31	19	17	1	2
Schools (K-12)	276	217	109	111	67	27	18 Wasau 6 Joint District	12	3
Schools (elementary)	193	168	74	78	51	22	14	8	1
Schools (junior high and middle)	36	31	17	22	9 (7 and 8)	3	2 (middle)	2 (junior high)	1
Schools (high and vocational)	26	18	8	9	7 (9-12)	1 senior 1 tech/voc	2 high	2	1
Students (elementary)	175,101	112,484	45,929	K: 1,407 40,579	22,502 (K-6)	7,287	4,312	4,200 (K-8)	498
Students (junior high and middle)	50,034	77,084	17,916	20,888	16,700	3,297	2,132	946	393
Students (high school and vocational)	59,232 (including 6,209 vocational)	n.a.	15,454	21,664	15,254	3,280	3,467	2,900 (9-12)	367
Number of students in K-12 system	284,367	193,150	79,299	84,538	41,000 (approx.)	13,800	9,911	7,333	1,258
Number of teachers	12,236	n.a.	2,799	3,030 (not including K)	1,884	615	498	128 (9-12)	67
Ratio of students to teachers	23/1	n.a.	28/1	28/1	28/1	n.a.	20/1	30/1	22/1
Number of classrooms	9,500	6,126 (plus 700 shops and labs)	4,471	3,342	n.a.	n.a.	450	n.a.	57

n.a.—figures not available.

What can you learn from an ACCOUNTANT?

Accountants make up the second largest field of professional employment for men, so finding one will not be difficult. They can be found wherever business, industrial, or governmental organizations are located. Most accountants do their accounting for the business or industrial firm they work with. Others are in public accounting as proprietors, partners, or employees of independent accounting firms, while the rest work for federal, state, and local government agencies.

Look in the phone book, write to accountant associations (for example, the American Institute of Certified Public Accountants, 666 Fifth Avenue, New York, New York 10019), call a hospital, a construction firm, or a large bakery; ask a lawyer for his accountant; check with your next-door neighbor.

There are different kinds of accountants you can look up. Even the smallest business, like a dress shop or toy store or hardware store, employs or uses some kind of accountant. Accountants can work in any of the following positions:

Assistant bookkeeper
Full-time bookkeeper
Chief accountant or office manager
Public accountant
Government accountant
Accounting specialist (including bookkeeping machine operator, cost accountant, internal auditor, systems expert, tax specialist, and investigator)

What are the differences among these jobs? Do any have to be certified (licensed)? How do you get certified? Do your duties change when you are certified?

Ask an accountant what you can learn about a business just by looking at what an accountant does. You can learn how much money the business is making or losing; you can learn what items of value the business owns, the amount of money in the bank, the amount owed to the business by customers, the amount of merchandise in the store, the amount of machinery and furniture. You can learn from the accountant how much money the business owes its creditors, how much it owes banks for mortgages and loans, the employees for wages, and the government for taxes.

The accountant can help you understand taxes as they relate to you and your family and the business he works for. He can help you understand the differences among local, state, and federal taxes and laws regulating business.

Ask to see the accountant's filing system, his graphs, his tables. How were they computed, and what do they mean? How do you do a balance sheet, an income statement, a cost study, a tax report? How have these procedures changed over the years?

If you talk to a public accountant, ask him how much he charges. How does he get his customers? Ask about advertising and public relations.

Ask an accountant whether he knows computer operations, programming, higher mathematics, and how this relates to what he does. (Also, see the section "Computer Programmer" in this book.) Ask an accountant if there are some seasons of the year that are busier than others and why. An accountant can introduce you to the use of mathematics, management, financial analysis and planning, the tax system and regulations, profits and losses—all the things that make the businesses in our country run.

What can you learn at an AIRPORT?

Airports are big, fascinating, and unique places. They are excellent for learning, even though they may not be too easy to get to. There's one near every city of any size.

Just wandering around the airport and observing is the best way to start learning there. Frequently, the airport will provide tours on request to individuals or groups. Someone in the airport administrator's office should be able to answer your questions and gain access for you to the areas that are prohibited to the public. The behind-the-scenes operations of the airport will be especially interesting.

You will do best to visit the airport when it will not be particularly busy, if you plan to ask questions and spend time talking to employees (weekends and holidays are definitely out). But peak periods are the most exciting times for just observing (weekends and holidays are definitely in). U.S. Air Force facilities and Naval Air Stations are often open to visitors as a part of Armed Forces Day celebrations, and these may well be of interest, if there are any near you.

The Busiest Airports in the United States

Airport	Total Passengers (in 1967)
Chicago—O'Hare	27,500,000
New York—J.F. Kennedy	19,900,000
Los Angeles	18,100,000
San Francisco	12,200,000
Atlanta	11,700,000
Miami	8,700,000
Washington, D.C.	8,500,000
New York—La Guardia	8,100,000
Boston	7,700,000
Newark	6,100,000
Detroit	5,800,000
Philadelphia	5,200,000
Denver	5,000,000
Pittsburgh	4,800,000
Saint Louis	4,500,000
Cleveland	4,400,000
Minneapolis	4,200,000
Seattle	3,800,000
Dallas	3,800,000
Houston	3,400,000
Kansas City	3,400,000
New Orleans	3,200,000
Honolulu	2,700,000
Las Vegas	2,600,000
Memphis	2,600,000

Here are some questions you might ask someone in the airport administrator's office, your tour guide, or any other employees you see working at the airport:

How big is the airport?
How many runways are there?
How long are the runways?
Can the airport service any size aircraft?
How many automobile parking spaces are provided?
How many passengers utilize the airport each year?
How many loading gates are there?
How many airplanes can land and take off in a single day?

How is the airport operated?
Who owns the airport?
What are the airport's sources of revenue?
Who manages the airport?
How are decisions made concerning airport operations?
What are the different jobs that must be performed?
How large a staff is required to operate the airport?

How does the ground side of the airport work?
How do people arrive at the airport?
How are cars parked and retrieved?
By what other means than automobiles may passengers arrive at the air terminal?
How are people transported through the air terminal?
How is congestion handled in the terminal building?
What is the longest distance a traveler may have to walk?
How is baggage transported through the terminal building?
How does the baggage handling system ensure that baggage reaches its proper destination?
To what extent is baggage handling automated?
What happens if baggage is misplaced or lost?
How is baggage returned to deplaning passengers?
How is the air terminal heated, ventilated, airconditioned?
What shopping facilities are located in the airport?
How is flight insurance sold to passengers?
How is the air terminal repaired and maintained?
How is required information displayed and made available to users?
How does cargo arrive at the airport?
How is cargo handled and transported through the airport?
What special passenger-handling provisions exist for disabled passengers?
What advertising exists in the airport?

How do airline ticket windows operate?
How are passenger reservations recorded, maintained, and processed?

Impact of new planes on terminal design

A study by American Airlines of the dimensions and capacities of new and developing aircraft, combined with projections of future traffic, resulted in a series of charts and diagrams visualizing new limits and area requirements that will apply to the new generation of airports. A selection of exhibits from this series follows. Not accounted for in the study, but perhaps capable of interpolation by inference, is Lockheed's giant C-5 Galaxy.

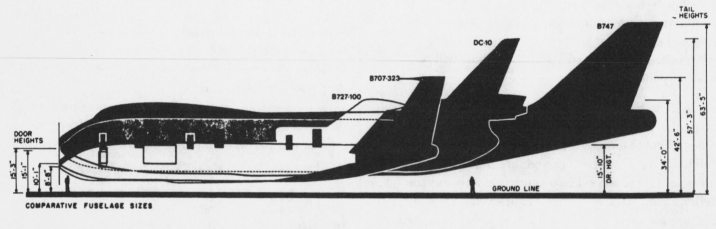

COMPARATIVE FUSELAGE SIZES

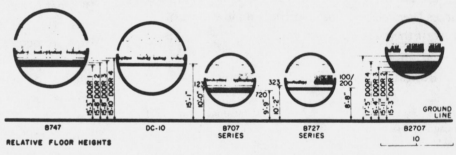

RELATIVE FLOOR HEIGHTS

How are tickets prepared?

What automated data-processing systems are employed by the airlines?

What special services do the airlines provide for passengers?

How is the price for different destinations determined?

What are the different rate schedules for different types of passengers?

How are the airline schedules determined?

What causes an airplane to be delayed in landing or take-off?

How are communications handled among the various members of the ground crew?

Who determines which cities will be served by which airlines?

What happens when a plane's departure is delayed?

How do pets travel by airplane?

What security provisions exist at an airport?

How are traffic jams handled?

What crime prevention and detection systems operate in the air terminal?

How do airlines discourage or guard against plane hijacking?

How are people prevented from entering restricted areas?

What happens when a bomb is reported to be on an airplane?

Why is security required at an airport?

How are emergencies handled at the airport?

What emergency first-aid and medical services are available?

What precautions are taken when a "wheels-up" landing is anticipated?

What fire-fighting equipment is maintained at the airport?

How are airplane fires brought under control?

How are passengers removed from disabled aircraft?

What civil defense procedures have been established?

How are emergency communications handled?

How often does a major emergency happen at the airport?

How does the air side of the airport operate?
How is the take-off and landing of airplanes controlled?

What happens in the control tower?

How is air traffic over the city regulated?

What is meant by the term "bird cage" with regard to air traffic?

How do airplanes land in bad weather?

How does radar work?

What happens when planes cannot land at the airport?

How is the decision made to close the airport?

How are snow and ice removed from the runways?

How often is it necessary to close the airport?

How do the runways work?

Do planes always land and take off in the same direction?

How are planes taxied to the air terminal?

How do pilots know their way around unfamiliar airports?

How are airplanes guided into the loading gates?

What traffic control systems regulate the movements of airplanes on the ground?

What happens when too many airplanes want to land at the same time?

What happens when airplanes have to wait for take-off?

How do airplanes communicate with the control tower?

How do passengers board the airplane?

How is baggage loaded onto the airplane?

How is cargo loaded onto the airplane?

How are meals and refreshments loaded onto the airplane?

How does the airplane communicate with the passenger agents?

How long does an airplane spend on the ground?

How are airplanes readied for flight?
Where are airplanes stored when not in use?

Where are airplanes repaired and serviced?

How do airlines decide which aircraft to use on different flights?

How do the airlines monitor where their planes are at any given point in time?

What preflight examinations does each plane undergo before taking off?

What periodic maintenance is performed on airplanes?

How are airplanes fixed?

What special test equipment is used in testing airplanes?

How are airplanes refueled?

Where is fuel stored at the airport?

How is fuel transported around the airport?

What kind of fuel do airplanes use?

How are airplanes cleaned?

How are meals prepared for the flight?

How are meals kept hot in transport?

What briefing does the crew undergo before the flight?

How is the flight plan determined for the trip?

How are weather conditions monitored before and during the flight?

How does an airplane operate?
What makes an airplane fly?

What different types of commercial aircraft are there?

What are the operating characteristics of different aircraft?

What is the difference between a propeller airplane and a jet?

How does a helicopter work?

How many passengers can an airplane carry?

How much cargo will a passenger plane hold?

What kind of crew does it take to operate an airplane?

How is the crew trained?

What are the qualifications for different crew jobs?

How many miles does an airplane fly in a year?

How many flights does an airplane make a day?

How are communications maintained while the plane is in flight?

What passenger services are available on board the aircraft?

How high do airplanes fly?

How fast can airplanes travel?

What makes an airplane crash?

How much does an airplane cost?

What emergency warning systems operate on an airplane?

How does the "automatic pilot" operate?

How does the airplane stay on course while in flight?

What does the flight engineer do?

How does an airplane "find" its destination airport?

What steps does the preflight check-out include?

How safe are airplanes?

Other sections in this book that might add to your knowledge of airplanes and airports are "Helicopter" and "Weather Forecasting."

What can you learn from an ARCHITECT?

Most of us never get to meet architects or understand what they do or how they do it. Yet we all experience the fruits of their labors when we use the buildings they design or admire or criticize their architecture. For good or bad, we are surrounded by architecture.

One of the more interesting offices you could visit would be an architect's office. Just to see the environment that people who design environments work in is worth the visit. Even more, architects tend to be articulate and interesting people—even offbeat at times. You can learn a great deal from them. An architect's office will reveal many tools and equipment you probably haven't seen before. Compare an architect's office to a lawyer's office or an insurance company office. How are they similar? In what ways are they different?

Look through the books and the magazines in the office. Watch drawings being prepared, and see how models are made. Ask the architect to explain how to read blueprints, and get him to show you a design problem he is currently working on. Trace the progress of a single design problem from beginning to end. There are approximately 37,000 registered architects in the United States and 83 Community Design Centers in 70 cities. For help in locating an architect to visit or for answers to your questions, contact the local chapter of the American Institute of Architects in or near your city or a Community Design Center.

Here are some questions to ask an architect about his profession:

How did you become an architect?
Where did you study architecture?
What courses did you study?
What was the hardest thing to learn?
What degrees do you have?
What training besides school did you have?
What kinds of tests and licenses are required to practice architecture?

How does an architect design?
What skills do you need to design buildings?
Do all architects do the same things?
Could you design any kind of building?
Are some buildings easier to design than others?
Do architects just design the outsides of buildings?
Do you especially like to design particular types of buildings?

What tools do you use to make architectural drawings?
How are drawings reproduced?
What is a blueprint?
Do you work with other professionals besides architects?
How do you know what building materials are available?
How do you know how people will use the building you design?
What regulations control your building design?
How do you determine the cost of a building?
Are all buildings designed by architects?

How does an architect earn his money?
Whom does an architect work for?
On what basis does an architect get paid for designing?
How does an architect get clients?
Do architects advertise?
How do architects earn their reputations?
What happens if the building you design doesn't get built?
Who owns the designs for a building?
What kinds of contracts do you use in your business?

Do you design things other than buildings?
Who designs bridges?
Who designs public spaces?
How do you treat the spaces around the buildings you design?
Do architects have anything to do with urban renewal?
What is a feasibility study?

What makes buildings stand up?
What is the difference among buildings made of brick, wood, steel, concrete, or stone?
How are buildings heated, ventilated, airconditioned?
Do you have any responsibilities for the success of a building?
How do foundations work?

Why do some buildings fall down?
What happens if the building falls down?
Can a building be considered a failure even though it stays up?
Do you ever forget to put something important into a building?
How do earthquakes affect buildings?
How does weather affect buildings?
What makes a building leak?
What makes buildings deteriorate?

What is the difference between a good building and a bad one?
Are some architects better than others?
Do architects win awards for designing buildings?
Who decides which buildings are good or bad?

Do architects differ on the subject of beauty?
What are the different architectural styles?
Are new buildings better than old ones?
What makes a building "modern"?

Is an architect a professional?
Are there professional journals and magazines for architects?
What professional societies exist for architects?
How do architects become members of professional societies?
What is the advantage of belonging to a professional society?
Do architects continue their education after leaving school?
Have things changed since you graduated from school?

What could I do to learn more about architects?
Are there particularly valuable things I could read?
Where could I write for more information?
Could you suggest other places or people I might visit?

See the sections "City Planning," "Hospital," "Sports Stadium," and "Zoning" in this book. What do architects do in these areas?

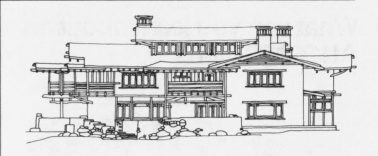

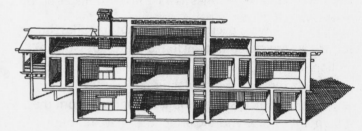

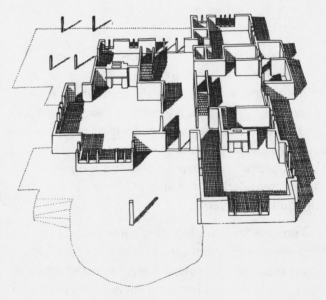

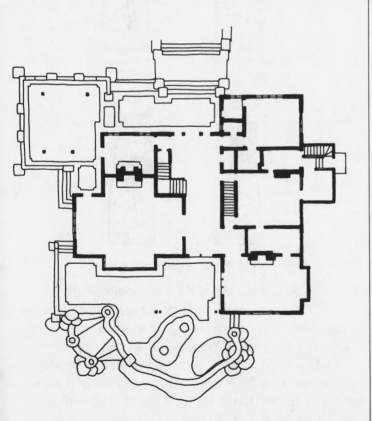

Gamble House

1908, Westmoreland Place, Pasadena, California, U.S.A.
Architect: Charles S. Green and Henry M. Green; Client: David B. Gamble. Elevation c. 1,000 feet. Fir structure, mahogany and teak interior.

Net:	7,384 sq. ft.
Gross:	8,534 sq. ft.
Open areas:	4,012 sq. ft.
Sleeping Porch:	400 sq. ft.
Net:	56,456 cu. ft.
Gross:	75,516 cu. ft.

What can you learn about an AUTOMOBILE?

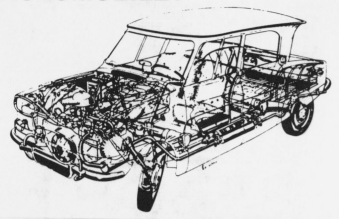

What's so wonderful about an automobile? We seem to take them for granted—for good or for bad. And, because there are so many all around us, we stop wondering about them. We no longer find it easy to distinguish their good points from their bad points and to consider alternatives to automobiles as a means of transportation.

In 1971 there were over 112 million automobiles, buses, and trucks registered in the United States, of which 93 million (about 90 percent) were passenger cars. The car industry is the largest manufacturing industry in our country. That makes automobiles important from the standpoint of jobs and the effect they have on our national economy. Each year we produce over 7 million new automobiles. Clearly, the automobile affects our lives intimately, whether or not we use them for getting from place to place.

Basically, every automobile is composed of an engine, transmission, drive shaft, differential, starter motor, steering gear, battery, brakes, wheels, seats, and a suspension system. All of these are put together to make a machine that converts energy in the form of gasoline into power for moving around. Any gas station attendant or auto mechanic can explain how this is done and how the different parts of the automobile work together. It's really quite remarkable.

Also, the process for manufacturing automobiles has been very important in pioneering techniques that have become central to our advanced technological society. The interchangeability of parts, the division of labor to allow assembly-line production, and cost reduction through mass production were all developed on a large scale by the automobile industry. A visit to an automobile plant where they make parts for automobiles or whole cars will demonstrate these important concepts and much more.

The effect of the modern automobile on our lives in cities is also very interesting. Consider, for example, that 25 to 40 percent of the land in our larger cities is devoted exclusively to the automobile (streets, parking lots and garages, repair shops, car washes, gas stations, and so on). In Los Angeles the figure is already over 67 percent. "Soon there will be no point in going anywhere," a transportation expert has observed, "because everywhere will be covered with concrete for getting there."

There is also a whole sector of goods and services that caters to the automobile user. These include drive-in movies, take-out restaurants, and drive-up windows in banks. Even mailboxes are sometimes designed so that a driver (or passenger) can mail a letter without getting out of his car.

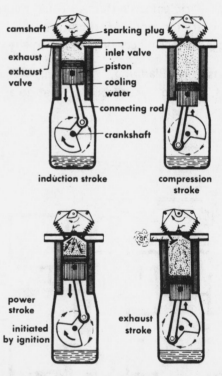

Operating principle of a four-stroke engine

Consider these facts about the automobile in our society: In 1971 the American motorist (collectively) drove 945 billion miles, which is roughly equivalent to driving to the sun and back 5,000 times or around the entire earth 38 *million* times. It is estimated that passenger cars are used for 90 percent of all recreation and vacation trips in the United States. In 1971, 110 million Americans (over half the total population) went on at least one vacation by car. There are almost 4 million miles of roads and streets in the United States (3,700,000). In 1970, 94 million gallons of motor fuel were consumed in the United States. From January to June 1971, over $36 billion worth of consumer installment credit was extended in the United States to buy cars. Federal funds for education for the whole year came to one-fifth of that amount. In 1969 there were 56,400 motor vehicle deaths, one-half the number of people who died of heart disease. One-half of highway fatalities are alcohol-caused.

Then, too, there are the traffic jams and the noise and air pollution caused by this vehicle of mobility on which we have become so dependent. Many people are now wondering if the problems caused by the automobile are worth its benefits. Walk around your city and think about it. Talk to a city planner, an ecologist, a transportation planner, or a city official. In this book, see the sections on "City Planning," "Gas Station," "Road Building and Repairing," and "Zoning."

The processes surrounding the automobile are many. Almost every day in every city, automobiles are being auctioned, bought, customized, driven, engineered, fixed, gassed up, hauled, inspected, licensed, lubricated, manufactured, overturned, parked, queued, raced, rented, simonized, towed, ticketed, unloaded, upholstered, viewed, washed, and waxed. You would have a hard time avoiding an opportunity to learn about one or more of these aspects of the automobile. Even if cars are not made in your city, chances are that parts of cars are made there or that cars are assembled nearby. Visit the places where these processes are taking place.

Make a list of questions about the things you want to learn concerning the automobile. Consider both what the automobile is and how it works. Then, think about the way it affects your life and the shape and quality of living in your city. Here are some people you might talk to:

Automobile salesman
Chauffeur
Taxicab driver
Truck driver
Automotive engineer
Automobile mechanic
Gas station attendant
Someone at the state department of motor vehicles
Someone who works at an automobile plant
Race car driver
Policeman
Collector of antique automobiles
Transportation planner

Stand on a street corner and watch the automobiles passing by, and ask yourself, "What's so wonderful about an automobile?"

What can you learn at a BAKERY?

One of America's largest food-processing employers is the bakery industry. About 85 percent of the workers in this industry are in establishments that produce perishable baked goods, such as cakes, breads, pies, rolls, and doughnuts. The others are employed by companies producing dry baked goods, like crackers, cookies, and ice cream cones.

There is some sort of bakery near you. It might be a (1) large wholesale bakery that sells to retail stores or hotels or restaurants; (2) bakery owned and run by a grocery chain; (3) home-service bakery that delivers to the customer's home; (4) central baking establishment of a company operating several retail bake shops; or (5) one of the thousands of single-shop retail bakeries.

Compare the different kinds and numbers of employees hired at a large establishment against your neighborhood corner bakery. In the larger organization ask for the community relations or public affairs department, the public relations office, or the personnel office. Often large bakeries conduct tours of the plant. For the small operation, just ask to speak to the owner or the manager.

Employees in the Shop
Although the smaller bakery does more individual work and often requires more skilled and creative workers, all bakeries will probably have some of the following kinds of employees involved in many different kinds of processes:
1. Production workers: Watch the machines these men load and unload, and inspect the results.
2. Mixers: What instruments are used to weigh the dough? How is the dough fermented? How long does the dough take to rise? How many times must the dough be fermented? What causes the dough to rise?
3. Dividermen: Do machines automatically divide the dough into certain sizes? What do the workers do? Is there much danger of accident to the employees?
4. Dough molders or molding machine operators: How are air bubbles removed from the dough? Why should they be removed?
5. Bench hands: Is the bread kneaded by hand or by machine? What is the purpose of kneading? Is there a special process for fancy-shaped bread or rolls?
6. Oven men: How high is the temperature for bread?
7. All-round bakers: In small bakeries, this person with helpers does all the tasks described here. The

helpers do a variety of chores, including cleaning up, washing dishes, greasing the pans, and removing bread from the pans.

8. Slicing and wrapping machine operators: How long does it take to wrap a loaf of bread in a plastic bag or paper and label it? Are the loaves given any final check before shipment?

9. Icing mixers: In a large bakery, is there any room for individual recipes? What kind of machines are used for mixing?

10. Hand icers: What kinds of special items require individual craftsmen to do icing?

There are then the workers employed in the storage, warehousing, and shipping departments. They can answer such questions as: How do you pack baked goods to ensure freshness? What additives are there to satisfy the same purpose? How are records of orders and deliveries kept to maintain an efficient organization?

Maintenance Occupations
Because of the multitude of machines, many electricians, machinists, and engineers are hired.

Sales and Driving Occupations
The driver-salesman is another important person in the bakery's operation. How does he get customers? How does a driver estimate what items his customer will want the following day? Who trains the driver-salesman?

Administrative, Clerical, and Professional and Technical Occupations
In large bakeries there are job classifications similar to those in any large company: supervisor, treasurer, comptroller, personnel officer, accountant, purchaser, and full clerical staff. Often there are also kitchen laboratories staffed with home economists and chemists that list new recipes. There may also be an advertising department.

How do you market a new product? How do you know what the public wants? Are there unions? What is the relationship between the union and the management? Where do the raw materials and the recipes come from? How many items are baked daily?

The small bakery offers special advantages to the observer. First of all, you can see all the operations readily. Also, many of the small retail establishments are ethnic bakeries. There you might be able to share in family recipes, learn the differences in ingredients between a German bakery and an Italian bakery, and learn about traditional baked goods (for example, hamantashin) and the different kinds of cakes or breads for various holidays.

What can you learn at a BANK?

Wherever you live, there's a bank nearby. There are different kinds of banks with different kinds of services, and you should first ask what kind of bank it is: a commercial bank, a mutual savings bank, a federal reserve bank. If you live in an area with more than one type of bank, compare the two in terms of their organization and their services. Also, compare the services of two banks within the same category. Do your banks provide any of the following? Do you know what they are?

Individual checking accounts
Letter of credit
Safe for money and valuables
Administration of trusts and personal estates
Loans to retail merchants, farmers, large industrial concerns
Loans to individuals for house purchase, automobiles, household items, or other personal loans
Revolving check credit plans
Credit cards
Travel services
Ticket agency
Drive-up windows
Special savings accounts
Traveler's checks

Who Works in a Bank?
Over 900,000 people are employed in banking organizations. Over two-thirds of these employees are involved in clerical jobs. (In 1966 commercial banks processed more than 20 billion checks—about 100 for every man, woman, and child in the country.) Some of these employees work as tellers or banks clerks, who handle thousands of checks, deposit slips, and other papers daily. Other employees include secretaries, stenographers, typists, receptionists, telephone operators, file clerks, mail helpers, card-tape converter operators, coding clerks, reconcilement clerks, verifier operators, data examination clerks, tape librarians, data processors, bookkeepers, shipping and receiving clerks, proof machine operators, collection clerks, check inscribers, and others whose functions are similar to those of clerical workers in other businesses.

There are also bank officers—president, vice-president, treasurer, comptroller, or other officials. Also attached to a bank may be lawyers, economists, accountants, statisticians, and public relations personnel, such as

THE FIDELITY BANK

Member Federal Deposit Insurance Corporation

TYPE OF LOAN DESIRED	☐ CASH-MATIC ☐ SURE CASH	☐ PERSONAL ☒ AUTO	☐ HOME IMPROVEMENT ☐ CONSOLIDATION	AMOUNT REQUESTED $ 1600	NUMBER OF MONTHS 24

NAME	JOHN DOE	SOCIAL SECURITY NO. 402-10-5621	DATE OF BIRTH	MONTH 4	DAY 10	YEAR 40	MILITARY STATUS Hon. DISCH.

SPOUSE'S NAME: MARY DOE | SOCIAL SECURITY NO. 301-26-5410 | MARITAL STATUS ☐ SINGLE ☐ DIVORCED ☐ WIDOWED ☒ MARRIED ☐ SEPARATED | NO. OF DEPENDENTS (NOT INCLUDING SPOUSE)

HOME ADDRESS (STREET AND NO.): 102 MAIN STREET #6 | EMPLOYED BY: HAPPY ENGINEERING | HOW LONG THERE? 4 YRS.

(CITY) HOMETOWN, MASS. (STATE) (ZIP) 00000 | HOW LONG THERE? 2 YRS. | EMPLOYER'S ADDRESS: 30 EAST STREET, (CITY) HOMETOWN, (STATE) MASS. (ZIP) 00000

☒ RENTING ☐ OWN ☐ OTHER ☐ BUYING ☐ LIVE WITH PARENTS | HOME PHONE NO. | BUS. PHONE NO. 123-4567 | POSITION ENGINEER | NET MONTHLY SALARY $ 425

LANDLORD OR MORTGAGE HOLDER NAME: JOHN SMITH | SPOUSE EMPLOYED BY: HOMETOWN PUBLIC SCHOOLS | HOW LONG THERE? 2 YRS.

ADDRESS: SAME AS ABOVE (CITY) (STATE) (ZIP) | ADDRESS (STREET AND NO.) 16 WEST ST, (CITY) HOMETOWN, (STATE) MASS. (ZIP) | NET MONTHLY SALARY $ 400

PURCHASE PRICE $ | BALANCE OF MORTGAGE $ | MONTHLY RENT OR MORTGAGE PAYMENT $ 200 | OTHER INCOME SOURCE NONE | NET MONTHLY AMOUNT $

SEND MAIL TO ☒ HOME ☐ BUSINESS	FIDELITY SERVICES YOU NOW USE		IF YOU OWN AN AUTOMOBILE (IF MORE THAN ONE GIVE INFORMATION ON NEWEST ONE)		
	CHECKING ACCOUNT NO. 546-030	SAVINGS ACCOUNT NO. 478-107	YEAR 68	MAKE, AND MODEL FORD FALCON	AMOUNT OWING $ 0
	OTHER SERVICES		FINANCED BY FIDELITY BANK		MONTHLY PAYMENT $

USE ONLY IF YOU ARE APPLYING FOR AN AUTOMOBILE LOAN

MAKE OF CAR CHEVROLET	MODEL NOVA	SERIAL NUMBER 128743	☒ NEW ☐ USED	YEAR 1972	CASH PRICE $ 2800

| ACTUAL CASH VALUE $ 2800 | LIFE INSURANCE ☒ YES ☐ NO | OPTIONAL EQUIPMENT ☒ POWER BRAKES ☒ POWER STEERING | ☒ AUTOMATIC TRANSMISSION | ☐ AIR CONDITIONING ☒ RADIO | |

TRADE IN & DOWN PAYMENT − 1400
BALANCE DUE $ 1400
INSURANCE PREMIUM + 200
TOTAL ADVANCE $ 1600

LIST ALL PRESENT AND CLOSED LOANS, INSTALLMENT OBLIGATIONS AND REVOLVING CREDIT ACCOUNTS NOT SHOWN ABOVE

CREDITOR	ADDRESS	ACCOUNT NO.	ORIGINAL AMOUNT	PRESENT BALANCE	MONTHLY PAYMENT
STURDY FURN. CO.	EAST BEND, MASS.	A4730	$ 1000	$ 200	$ 25
			$	$	$
			$	$	$
			$	$	$

REFERENCES—RELATIVES NOT LIVING WITH YOU (WE DO NOT CONTACT)

RELATIONSHIP	NAME	ADDRESS
FATHER	HARRY DOE	46 DAY ST., WEST BEND, MASS. 01730
SISTER	SUSIE DOE JONES	189 SOUTH ST. #4C, NEW YORK, NEW YORK 10002

FOR BANK USE ONLY			I affirm that each of the answers given to the foregoing questions is true and correct and authorize anyone mentioned to furnish you such information as you may require in connection with this application.
SOURCE	BRANCH	APPLICATION #	
APPROVED BY	DATE	ACCOUNT #	8/1/72 DATE John R Doe SIGNATURE

photographers, writers, and printers. Finally, there are the maintenance personnel, guards, elevator operators, and other service personnel.

Before talking to personnel at the bank, you might want to write to the following address for information about the banking industry and general information about banking opportunities:
American Bankers Association
Personnel Administration and Management
Development Committee
90 Park Avenue
New York, New York 10016

You might also want to go to your library to look up the definitions of different categories of banks. When it is time to visit, ask for the branch manager or someone in the personnel or public relations office.

Ask how many employees there are and what they do. If you know exactly what kind of information you want, ask to speak directly to an individual in that department; for example, if you are interested in the kind of advertising the bank uses, ask for the public relations office.

Open a Savings Account

Follow the paper work of each of the people who have something to do with your account. How are the files kept? Are transactions written or electronically recorded? If the bank burns down, is there another record of your account? Do you have a passbook or is a statement just sent to you at designated intervals? Is your signature on your records? Is it invisible to the naked eye?

Follow your money. Where does your money go once you have opened your account? Is it locked up in a big safe? Does the bank keep all the money its depositors put in? What is your money used for—loans, buildings, investment? How many people are involved with your one deposit?

Look at your deposit slip and your application form. Who designed them? Is there a special form every bank must use? If so, who legislates that? Are there laws governing who may open an account and who may not or laws about who may withdraw money from an account? Who establishes these laws and who enforces them?

Why should you put your money into a bank? What is interest? What are the different kinds of savings accounts?

Look at the bank. Is the bank designed in a certain way? Was special consideration given for customer movement? During what hours is the bank open? Are some hours busier than others? If so, why? Is it because it is payday or just before a holiday?

What are checking accounts and loans? What are they used for and how do you get one? How come a store will accept a check instead of cash for an item you want to buy? Will any piece of paper do or must you use an official check? What's a traveler's check, a money order? When you pay by check, how does a shop owner know you have money in the bank?

Why do people go to one bank rather than another? What services draw the most people with the most money? What is meant by the Federal Reserve system? What is the American Institute of Banking? Is there one in your area? What is the gold standard? (See the section "Money" in this book for answers to some of these questions and hints on how to find the answers to others.)

The bank is an excellent place to learn about the general operations of a large company. It is also a good place to understand our money system, how it works, and how it affects you daily.

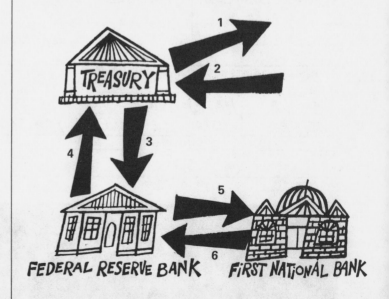

1. Treasury sells gold. 2. Takes check from buyer of gold. 3. Deposits check in Federal Reserve Bank. 4. Redeems gold certificate. 5. Federal Reserve collects check from bank on which drawn, by 6. Deducting the amount from bank's reserve account. Thus, when the Treasury sells gold, bank reserves are decreased.

What can you learn from a BRICKLAYER?

"Bricklayers are getting scarce." This was the reply given to me when I questioned a former bricklayer about his trade. I had seen him working at a construction site and stopped to admire his work. (To find out what some of the other learning resources at any construction site are, read the section "Construction Site" in this book.)

"The large buildings being built today are not using brick and block anymore. If you want to see brick work being done and talk with men in the trade, the best place to find one would probably be an apartment complex or the construction site of row houses.

"Training for brick work is offered at vocational schools, and a lot more is learned on the site when you're an apprentice worker. I started as a hod carrier. That's the man who mixes the mortar and then carries the mortar and brick or block over to the men doing the actual laying of the brick. When you mix the mortar you get a real feel for it; you learn to tell if it is too heavy or too thin and what to do to make it thicker. After you get a feel for the materials, the boss puts you on to odds and ends of work like doing the 'back up' units. That means you learn to use the trowel and spread the mortar and lay the brick on. You learn about levels and how to make a corner. You do your learning on the back up parts, not the finished outside wall. When you really get proficient, you work on the outside walls.

"There are a lot of fine examples of brick work around this city—lots of types and styles that have disappeared with their makers. Like the Friends' Meeting House at 12th Street. That kind of brick work I think is called Flemish Bond. That refers to a certain way the bricks are laid; it has to do with the way they interlock, I think.

"There are many, many ways to handle bricks, like the Rolok walls. That's what you often see under windows. It's a way of keying the bricks to make a pattern. The joints, or places where the bricks come together, can also be handled in different ways. For instance, the headers (the end of the brick) can be flush or plain-cut, V-shaped, or concave."

I asked him where I could find illustrations of the different kinds of brick work he was describing, and he directed me to a book on architecture. Here are some examples of the many different kinds of brick work.

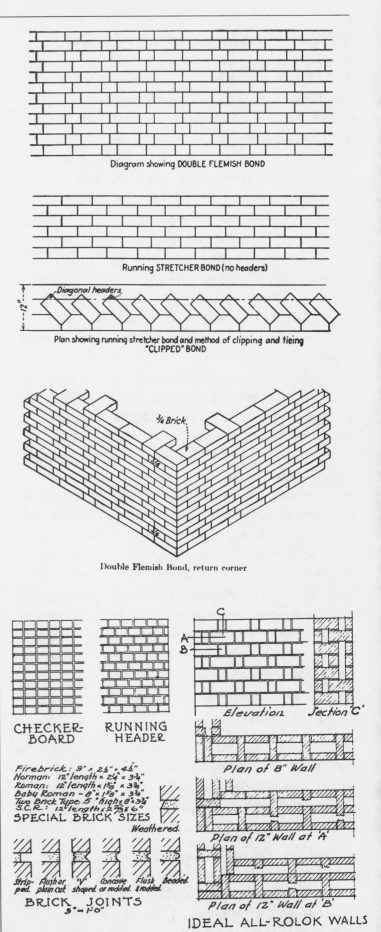

Diagram showing DOUBLE FLEMISH BOND

Running STRETCHER BOND (no headers)

Plan showing running stretcher bond and method of clipping and tieing "CLIPPED" BOND

Double Flemish Bond, return corner

CHECKER-BOARD

RUNNING HEADER

Firebrick: 9" x 2½" x 4½"
Norman: 12" length x 2¼ x 3¾"
Roman: 12" length x 1⅝ x 3¾"
Baby Roman " 8" x 1⅝" x 3¾"
Two Brick Type-5 "high x 8"x 3¾"
S.C.R.: 12" length x 2⅝ x 6"
SPECIAL BRICK SIZES

Weathered.

Stripped. Flush or plain cut. "V" shaped. Concave or rodded. Flush & rodded. Beaded.
BRICK JOINTS
3"-1'-0"

Elevation   Section 'C'

Plan of 8" Wall

Plan of 12" Wall at 'A'

Plan of 12" Wall at 'B'

IDEAL ALL-ROLOK WALLS

What can you learn from a BUTCHER?

Fred has been a butcher for twelve years and says he could tell you "everything you want to know" about the trade. I met him in the small meat market near where I work. When I asked the first butcher I saw behind the counter if I could ask him a few questions, he directed me at once to Fred. Fred is the "meat man" and says the best training comes from actually handling the meat and from the meat itself. He thinks that butcher school is largely a waste of time ("You don't cut nothing in butcher school—guys out of there don't know pork from lamb") and that you learn the trade only when you start working. He himself received no school training ("You don't learn nothing about it from books") but started out in a chain store twelve years ago. He outlined for me the grades of beef, his specialty —prime, choice, good, commercial, utility, standard— and told me what each means. Grade, he explained, means how, where, and how much the cow was fed. Lamb, on the other hand, is all one grade. Pork, too, is usually one grade, but again it depends on how, where, and how much the pig was fed. Fred added that there is a shortage of meat cutters, even though a 40-hour a week apprentice makes $240 a week. A meat cutter (as Fred described it, "No slaughter. We get the meat once it's dead") specializes in meat, chicken, fish, or deli (lunch meat, cold cuts, potato salad—Fred didn't have much respect for this position). I got the impression that the meat man was the top man. Each step means different pay. Of the 1,000 butchers in this city, Fred said, about 900 are unionized and work in small markets like this one, wholesale or retail stores, hospitals, hotels, and in the big chain stores.

When I asked about meat and consumer protection, Fred explained that years ago powder, seasoning, and chemicals were sometimes added to the meat to help it retain its color and make it look fresh but that now strict governmental regulations prevent this.

As Fred and I talked (Fred in blood-spattered apron and white coat and me across the deli case from him leaning against the glass), Lou, the "chicken man," came over and, while Fred took care of a customer, told me about his specialty. After the chickens are eviscerated, that is, all cleaned with the liver, gizzard, heart, and neck in a plastic bag inside, he cuts them up into legs, breasts, and wings. He makes five-pound bags of legs and breasts, a special item of the store, and puts the rest out for sale separately. He told me they get their chickens from a packing house, which gets them from farmers. He, too, explained grade to me, this time of chicken. Chicken, he said, is usually either A or B grade; these include broiler (a two-pound chicken at two cents a pound), fryer (a three-pounder), capon (a "denatured" rooster, usually five to nine pounds and used as a roasting chicken), stewers (which, at the time we talked, were "too expensive" and the store was not carrying them), duck (which they get when the price is right), as well as cornish hens. Steak, he told me, keeps less than a week, while chicken can stay safely refrigerated for one week. He rotates the refrigerator case (that deli case I was leaning on) daily so that yesterday's chicken is sold first today. Prices for all the meat and fish, Lou said, come from a "market sheet," which comes to the boss in the mail—Lou didn't know from where.

Business was picking up so Lou had to go, but everyone I met there was happy to pause when he had the time and talk and tell about what he did. Next time I visit, I'm going to try to get on the other side of that deli case to see that Pennsylvania beef and those Iowa pork loins close up. As Fred said, "It's up to the individual what he learns."

What can you learn about CANDY MAKING?

Mom used to hide the candy way up on the top of the bookcase, where I couldn't reach it. I remember thinking how neat it would be to be grown up and have tons of candy whenever I wanted. I figured that if I worked in a candy store, I could spend all day picking at chocolate-covered cherries, gumdrops, and enormous, shiny lemon sticks.

Someone told me that in some candy stores the people don't just sell the candy, they make it as well. I imagined myself working in one of those stores someday, mixing up caramel and nuts, coconut and marshmallows, and creating all kinds of wild combinations. But it takes forever to grow up, and when you *really* love candy, it's awfully hard to wait. So I looked in the Yellow Pages. And under a listing of "Candy—Confectionery, Retail," I found a store that advertised homemade candy and that wasn't too far from my home.

Before I even reached the store, I could smell the cocoa. There were some people shopping in the store. After they left, the woman behind the counter asked me what I wanted, and I explained that I wanted to learn about candy making. She took me through a door into the back of the store where there was another woman stirring a huge pot on a stove. Mrs. Wimble—that was the stirrer—said she'd be happy to let me watch. She told me to guess what was in the pot. It was easy—nothing smells as pungent as peppermint. She used a big candy thermometer, which told her when the sugary mixture was just hot enough, and then she began to drip swirls of the peppermint onto a big slab of marble.

"Have one," she said. It was terrific. While she worked, Mrs. Wimble explained that many candy stores get

their candy from factories, and that the name and address of the factory is printed on every box. So any time I wanted to see a really big operation, I should go to a factory, where candy is made by machines, instead of people.

When the peppermints were done, she picked up a huge basket of strawberries and sat down with them next to a pot of melted chocolate.

"Chocolate-dipped strawberries are very perishable," she said. "They must be eaten within a day or two." One by one, she dipped the berries in the chocolate and stuck them on toothpicks to dry. I'd never heard of putting strawberries and chocolate together. I wanted to make one myself, but Mrs. Wimble said she couldn't afford any mistakes. She suggested that I try my own candy making at home.

"Look up candy in a cookbook," she said. "Start with something easy, like fudge. Then work your way up." She gave me lots of hints on candy making. For example, you can't make good hard candies in a moist, hot atmosphere—they get sticky and sugary. She also told me to be sure the pot I used would hold four times as much as the ingredients, so that the syrup wouldn't boil over the top. Candies that call for butter, cream, milk, chocolate, or molasses are apt to burn if they're not stirred continuously the whole time they're cooking. Most of the ingredients I'd need would probably be in the kitchen already. The only investment I'd have to make would be for the candy thermometer, which the cookbook would tell me how to use.

Before I left, Mrs. Wimble gave me her peppermint drop recipe:

2 cups of sugar
1/4 cup of corn syrup
1/4 cup of milk
1/4 teaspoon cream of tartar
Cook and stir slowly until the candy thermometer reads 238 degrees. Cool slightly. Beat 'til creamy. Flavor with 1/2 teaspoon peppermint and add some food coloring if you want. Drop from a teaspoon onto waxed paper.

I was in such a hurry to get home and start, I almost forgot the bag of candy Mrs. Wimble gave me when she said good-bye.

What can you learn from a CARPENTER?

In order to learn from a carpenter, your first task will be to find one. This can be done in several ways. You can (1) ask a friend if he or she knows a carpenter, (2) look for one at a construction site, (3) hang around a lumberyard, (4) look one up in the telephone book under "Carpenters," (5) call or visit a local carpenters' union, (6) visit a cabinet shop, or (7) listen for the sound of wood being sawed. Even if the carpenter you succeed in finding is not very talkative you can learn a lot by just watching. But chances are the carpenter you meet will willingly share his knowledge with you. I haven't met a carpenter yet who didn't enjoy talking about his trade.

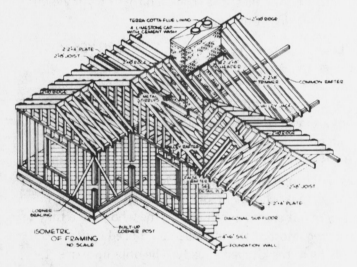

A good strategy is to start by asking him where he learned his skills and how he decided to become a carpenter. Are there schools where carpenters learn their trade? Do carpenters take on and train apprentices? How does the carpenter's union operate? Next you can ask him to demonstrate how he uses his tools. If you can get the carpenter to describe what each of his tools is and how each works, you are off to a flying start. Make sure you get a chance to watch him work and use his tools—that's the best part.

Find out how he measures in different kinds of situations. Ask him to explain the concepts of "tolerance," "straight," "true," and "plumb" for you. See how he makes joints and how he turns corners with wood (therein lies a great deal of the art of carpentry), and

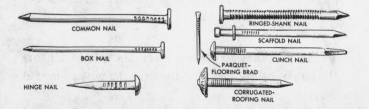

ask him to tell you about the wood he's working with. What are its characteristics? Find out how he selects particular woods for particular jobs. How does he know which screw sizes and what nails are appropriate? Can he build without using nails or screws? See if he will let you try out his tools, but be prepared for a possible *no* answer. The carpenter's tools are his best friends, and an amateur can all but ruin an otherwise fine instrument by using it improperly. Part of the key to getting a difficult carpentry job done well is having the right tool for each job and knowing how to use it.

Some of the most interesting things to watch the carpenter doing include the following:

Making drawers
Hanging a door
Building stud walls
Finishing dry wall or sheetrock
Making cabinets
Building a roof
Laying a floor
Restoring old woodwork
Building a set of stairs
Installing a window frame and jamb

If after watching the carpenter, you should decide to try your hand at woodworking, start small and be prepared for mistakes and frustration. The carpenter will have probably made the job look a lot easier than it really is. And, although carpentry isn't difficult, there's a natural tendency for novices to underestimate the skill required to do it well. This could be a good place to augment experiential learning with some basic texts.

After learning from a carpenter you may want to extend your experience by watching other specialized woodworkers display their skills. For example, find a furniture maker or factory and learn how furniture is made. Perhaps you can locate an architectural model maker and watch scale models of buildings and urban designs being made. An industrial designer who makes scale models of prototype designs would also be fascinating. Or find an exhibit designer who builds museum displays or exhibits. If there are theaters nearby, you can stop in and see how carpentry skills are used to make theater sets. How many other places in the city can you find where carpentry skills are being applied in special ways?

A good carpenter can drive a 6d (penny) nail with three strokes: the first to start the nail, the second to drive it all but in, and the third to set it. Wow!

What can you learn at a CEMETERY?

Death is nothing to us, since when we are, death has not come, and when death has come, we are not.
—Epicurus Diogenes Lairtius (born in 412 B.C.)

But when we are not, we leave our sign in a cemetery for others to see. Find a cemetery (look in the Yellow Pages, try next to a church, ask a clergyman, call City Hall, call a funeral home, read death notices in a newspaper) and walk around.

Watch the people who come there, and begin to think of all the people, in addition to the deceased and his friends and relatives, who may be involved for the death of each person buried in this one cemetery:

1. Undertaker
2. Clergyman
3. Tombstone engraver
4. Funeral director
5. Embalmer
6. Grave digger
7. Cemetery maintenance crew
8. Gardeners and security personnel
9. Florist
10. Caterer
11. Casket maker
12. Organist
13. Coroner
14. Cemetery architects and designers
15. Doctor
16. Newspaper writer
17. Personnel in City Hall's Vital Statistics Department
18. Personnel at the morgue
19. Personnel at the crematorium
20. Sympathy card publishers and staff

What is the role of each of the above? How has it changed over the years, and how does it differ depending upon money paid for services?

Watch funeral parties arrive at the cemetery and compare them. Who arrives first? Is there a pecking order of cars? Are people dressed a certain way? What is considered to be proper decorum, or behavior, in this situation? What religious rites take place and what is their significance? Do they tell you anything about the people's religious or ethnic backgrounds? What are the various roles of the grieving and their friends and relatives?

Look at the layout of the cemetery. Who designed it? When was it laid out? Have the needs and therefore the layout changed? Is there a minimum amount of space needed for each dead person? Who owns the cemetery? Are there zoning ordinances? Check with the water department or an engineer for rules governing drainage pipes. Is there a certain pervasion of one color throughout the cemetery? Are there flowers around? What kind? Are they left on special occasions or holidays?

Look at tombstones and notice especially the dates on them. Has the material they are made from changed? What has been the effect of time and weather? Have epitaphs changed? Look at tombstones from the same year. Are there differences in stone or style among them? Did people seem to die at a younger age a hundred years ago? Is there one year that has many deaths? If so, check in City Hall for records of a plague or epidemic. Look at the architecture of large tombs. Can you distinguish differences in religion, social and economic class, and time from the words and the materials? Who composes the message on the tombstone?

How much does death cost, and where can you die? How do you buy a plot, and who buys a plot? For how much? Can you get into a cemetery without a reservation? Are there laws against discrimination? Are there such things as public and private cemeteries? How is a body shipped? Do you have to be a U.S. citizen to be buried here? What laws govern the digging up of a body? Is there insurance to cover burial costs, or can it be covered and paid for by a will?

Who visits a cemetery? What do people do in a cemetery when they visit? Is the cemetery only open at certain times? Is there much vandalism?

What can you learn from a CHILD?

Being a child is not easy, you know. I keep changing. Just as I get used to some new part of my body, I find another. You can learn a lot from me. Those first years when I am an infant, you should watch me grow; my muscles and limbs change; I learn to hear and recognize my favorite animals and people; I learn to sit as my back strengthens. When I am young, you could see how my eating habits change, how my need for sleep changes, how I cry for special reasons with special cries.

Talk to my mother, my pediatrician. Compare me to others exactly my age and mark our growth; compare me to what the books say. What month was it when I first saw that mobile? When was the first time I grabbed for it? The first time I could take it to my mouth? The first time I dropped it and was able to remember where I dropped it and then put it where I wanted it?

Look at my eyes and the shape of my head. Compare the proportions of the different parts of my body with the proportions of yours. Watch how my hair and fingernails grow. Did I crawl before I walked? Did I stand before I crawled?

Watch other people's reactions to me. Listen to how they talk to me. Do people talk to me the way they would talk to you, or do they use a special language or tone of voice? Do people bring me up to them, do they come down to me, or do they tower over me?

Where can you find me? I'm next door, at your aunt's, in the room next to yours, at the baby doctor's, in the day nursery, in a kindergarten room, in the park with my mother or babysitter. I can be found in strollers, cribs, playpens, tubs, swingamatics, backpacks, bassinets, and in people's arms.

I'm really pretty wonderful!

What can you learn at CITY HALL?

City Hall belongs to you and the other citizens of your city. Too often, it is viewed as an obstacle and a constraint rather than the resource that it truly is.

Many cities publish a directory that lists the departments that make up the city government and their responsibilities. Often, guided tours of City Hall are available on a regular basis or on request. Your local ward leader or city councilman can assist you in gaining access to the information or departments that interest you.

You owe it to yourself to visit the legislative branch of your city's government while it is in session to see how laws are debated and enacted. And you should also get acquainted with the departments and agencies in City Hall by finding out what they do and how they do it.

It may be true that "you can't fight City Hall." But you can certainly learn a lot there. For example, in each of the following departments you can learn:

Civil Defense Department
What types of disasters have been planned for
How the city will operate in the event of a major disaster
What emergency communications systems exist
Which people have responsibilities during a disaster
Where emergency supplies have been stored
Which buildings and shelters have been designated for use in an emergency
How much it costs to be prepared for emergencies
What would happen if there were no emergency preparations
How different disasters would affect the city

Finance Department
How much money it costs to run the city
How the city maintains and monitors its budgets
What the difference is between an operating budget and a capital budget
What the city spends its money for
Where the money comes from
How the city borrows money
What banks the city uses
How much money the city has at any given time
How the city seeks additional funds from state and federal government

Procurement Department
How the city lets contracts for work, services, or materials
How the city buys property

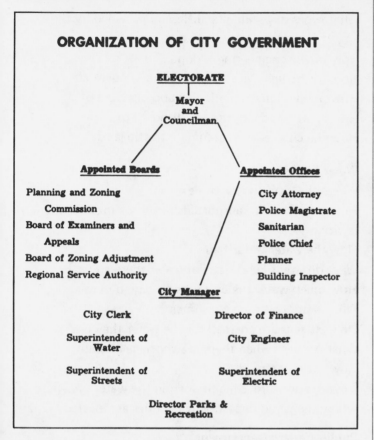

ORGANIZATION OF CITY GOVERNMENT

ELECTORATE

Mayor
and
Councilman

Appointed Boards

Planning and Zoning
    Commission
Board of Examiners and
    Appeals
Board of Zoning Adjustment
Regional Service Authority

Appointed Offices

City Attorney
Police Magistrate
Sanitarian
Police Chief
Planner
Building Inspector

City Manager

City Clerk   Director of Finance

Superintendent of   City Engineer
    Water

Superintendent of   Superintendent of
    Streets   Electric

Director Parks &
Recreation

How the city obtains its required supplies
Where and how the city stocks its supplies
What testing laboratories the city operates
How the city sets standards for the things it buys
How the city picks its purchasing sources
How the city maintains inventories on the items it
stocks

Law Department

What legal services are required by the city
What happens if the city must go into court
How bills and laws are written for the city council
What records must be maintained by the city
What operations the city is forbidden to engage in
How citizens can redress grievances against the city

Collections Department

What taxes the city depends on for its revenues
How taxes are collected
What happens when someone is delinquent in paying
taxes
What license fees are collected by the city
What additional sources of revenue the city has
How the city collects money from parking meters

Commerce Department

How the city attempts to attract industry
How the city seeks conventions and attractions
How the city provides for ceremonies

What public information services the city maintains
What steps the city takes to promote itself
How the city pursues its economic development ob-
jectives
How the city "competes" with other cities
What airports, piers, museums, and convention centers
are operated by the city

Fire Department

What equipment the city owns and maintains for fight-
ing fires
How many fire stations and firemen there are in the
city
What it costs to protect the city from fire
How the fire reporting system operates
How decisions are made regarding the deployment of
fire-fighting equipment
What it costs to build a fire station
Where the city buys its fire trucks
How the city seeks to prevent fires before they start
What rescue services are provided by the city

Licenses and Inspections Department

The range of licenses issued by the city
Why the city finds it necessary to issue licenses
How licenses are issued
Why licenses are revoked or not renewed
How the city building code operates
How the city zoning ordinance operates
How the city housing code operates
How the city plumbing code operates
How the city maintains its inspection procedures
What happens when violations to the various codes
are reported

Police Department

How many police stations and squad cars the city main-
tains
What it costs to protect the city from crime
How traffic is dealt with by police
How the city operates its jails
What happens when crimes are reported
How the city detectives operate
What protection services the city offers
How the city guards its property
How the police emergency communication system oper-
ates
What rights alleged criminals have
How crime rates have changed over time
What educational services are provided by the police
department
How police records are maintained

How the police department works with other law enforcement agencies—local, state, and federal

How the crime laboratory operates

How citizen complaints against the police are handled

Public Health Department

What health and health information services the city provides

How the city maintains health records

What health inspection procedures are employed by the city

What mental health services are provided by the city

How the city seeks to maintain clean air and water

What hospitals the city operates

What it costs the city to provide health services

What health hazards the city must guard against

What functions the medical examiner serves

Public Property Department

How the city acquires and disposes of property

How the city maintains public property

What it costs to maintain public property

How the city plans its new buildings

How the city builds new facilities

Records Department

What records must be maintained by the city

How the city keeps its records and makes them accessible

Which records are of historical significance

How deeds are recorded

How the city designs and maintains its forms and record-keeping systems

What it costs the city to maintain its records

Recreation Department

What recreation facilities and services the city provides

How the city plans parks and playgrounds

What cultural opportunities are provided by the city

What it costs the city to provide its recreation services

How citizens can request the recreation services they want

Streets Department

How many miles of paved streets the city has

What a street costs

How the city provides lighting for its streets

How the city repairs and cleans its streets

What it costs to clean the city's streets

How the city designs and builds new streets

How the city determines standards for its streets

How surveying is performed for the city

What types of parking facilities are provided by the city

How traffic engineering is done

How traffic lights are constructed and operated

How public refuse is collected and disposed of

How abandoned vehicles are disposed of

How the city seeks to eliminate traffic jams

Water Department

Where the city's water comes from

How the water is transported from its source to where it is processed

How the water is purified

What different conditions of water there are

How much water the city uses by day, by year

What water costs the consumer

How citizens are charged for the water they use

What happens when there is a shortage of water

How water is stored

How the pressure is maintained in the water system

Where the water department facilities are located

Public Welfare Department

Which residents of the city receive assistance in the form of welfare

How people qualify for welfare payments

How credentials are checked

Where the city obtains the funds it dispenses for welfare

What the city's welfare budget is per year

How much money it costs to live at a minimal level in the city

What forms of assistance in addition to money are available

How the welfare department selects its staff

Personnel Department

How many employees work for the city

The salary range for city employees

How Civil Service regulations are set up and operated

Why the Civil Service System was created

How personnel tests are designed and administered

What qualifications are required for different city jobs

How complaints from employees are handled

How employees' performance is reviewed

City Council

How many representatives are elected to the city's legislative branch of government

How legislative decisions are made

What procedural rules govern the council's operation

What committees serve the council

How citizens are encouraged to participate in decision making

How the city council reviews the performance of the operating departments

How much councilmen earn for their job

How councilmen may be censured for wrongdoing

How laws and bills are drafted

How council proceedings are recorded and maintained

How the council releases information to the press

City Controller's Office

To whom the controller is responsible

How the controller is selected

How the various departments that collect and dispense funds are audited

What happens when discrepancies in a department's books are found

District Attorney's Office

How the city prosecutes criminals

What it takes to prepare a case for court

How the DA works with the police department

How special investigations are handled

How many court cases the city pursues each year

What it costs the city to take a criminal to court

City Planning Department

How the city plans its growth and development

How information is collected and analyzed

How base maps for the city are maintained and updated

How state and federal programs become available to the city

How the city's Workable Program operates

What zoning is and how it is used

How the city's Capital Improvements Program is prepared and updated

What skills are required to plan for a city

How the City Planning Department's decisions are implemented

What the relationship is between the City Planning Department and other city departments

How the city reviews the plans of private developers

How the city produces its Master Plan

Redevelopment Authority

How urban renewal operates

What happens when homes must be displaced for clearance projects

How much money the city receives from the federal government for redevelopment purposes

What the city's goals are in pursuing redevelopment

Mayor's Office

How the mayor relates to the various city departments

What functions the mayor serves

How the mayor selects the city officers for whom he is responsible

How the mayor spends his time

Transportation Department

What transportation services are provided by the city

What it costs to maintain the city's transportation system

Where the city obtains its transportation equipment

How the city plans its transportation system

How the city obtains the revenue to support the transportation system

Sanitation Department

How the city handles its wastes

What happens to wastewater from the streets

How wastes are treated

Where the end product of waste treatment is disposed of

How the city's waste treatment facilities are controlled by state and federal government

How the city raises funds to build new waste treatment facilities

How old the city's sewer system is

How the sewerage system is maintained and repaired

How many miles of sewers the city operates

What advanced technologies of waste treatment are available

What it costs to handle the city's wastes

Public Affairs Department

What city information is made available to citizens

How the city organizes its public affairs department

What the differences are among departments, boards, advisory boards, commissions, and authorities

How administrative decisions are made for the city as a whole

How the city reports its progress to its citizens

Many, many processes in your city are somehow connected to City Hall. Some processes that are explored in more detail in this book are "City Planning," "Voting," and "Zoning." The section entitled "Ward Leader" should also expand your knowledge of what goes on in City Hall.

What can you learn about CITY PLANNING?

At first, I found it hard to believe that my city was actually being planned. But that's what I had heard. It's hard to believe because of all the old dilapidated buildings, the constant traffic jams, the noise and air pollution, and the obvious need for more public facilities, like parks and playgrounds, health centers, schools, and new buildings.

Well, I'm not the type who can sit back and believe something just because people tell me it's true. I have to find things out for myself. So I decided to take a trip down to City Hall and find out what city planning was all about.

As it turns out, there's a whole city agency called the City Planning Commission, which does the city's planning. The name of this city department varies widely from city to city, sometimes called the City Planning Department or City Planning Board or a similar variation, but they're all just about the same. In larger cities, there's a technical staff of professional city planners who do all the analysis, design, and planning. Then there's the body of decision makers, usually about seven or nine, who are appointed by the mayor and who serve without pay. It is this group's task to review the work done by the technical staff and to actually make the decisions on behalf of the public interest. The decision-making body usually meets only every two weeks or once a month, but the staff is always working at City Hall. In smaller towns and cities, where the work load and budget for planning functions are small, there may only be a decision-making body without a permanent professional staff.

I wasn't surprised that the city planners on the staff were more than willing to take time to meet with me and explain how the city plans for its future. After all, the members of the city planning staff are public servants, and I am a part of the public. Besides, I soon learned how important the role of citizen involvement is to the whole planning process. The city planners actually need people like you and me to become knowledgeable and interested in the problems and opportunities confronting our city and to play an active role in helping to make planning decisions.

I learned about the history of city planning and that it is a relatively recent phenomenon in this country. Planning as a municipal function did not begin to receive wide-scale acceptance until the late 1930s, and even then it was slow to catch on. I was told that the city depends heavily on funds from the state and federal governments for the implementation of its programs. I saw how analysts take information from the census and from many other sources and analyze it to understand better the conditions and trends in the city.

I was fascinated by the colored maps that describe how every single parcel of land in the city is being used, and I was amazed to find out that the city planners had made a map of what the city would look like in twenty-five years. And they told me about the programs they were initiating to make their plans come true.

I learned how to read different kinds of maps and how to understand aerial photographs. At the City Planning Commission they maintain a file of a wide range of maps at different scales that contain many different types of analytic information. There are also different base maps for every area in the city that can be used for many kinds of planning activities.

I asked a lot of questions and found out how planners use public housing, zoning, and urban renewal programs, among many others, to improve the quality of life in the city. Actually, the City Planning Commission is only one of many public agencies that are involved in planning and development activities. There's also a redevelopment agency that implements the U.S. Department of Housing and Urban Development programs on a day-to-day basis. A Regional Planning Agency undertakes planning for the entire metropolitan area and coordinates the individual plans of the cities and counties in its area. There are state departments, too, which work closely with the local and regional agencies. For specialized planning activities, like roads and highways, mass transit, industrial development, and housing development, there are also public or quasi-public organizations formulating and implementing short- and long-range plans for the future. Indeed, coordinating the activities of all these agencies and organizations is a considerable task.

There's a lot more to city planning that just being concerned with the design of buildings and the way the city looks from an aesthetic point of view. The real issues are how the city can provide services and amenities for its citizens, whether it can operate efficiently within the fiscal resources available to it, and how it can change as the needs and wishes of people change. Each year the city has only a limited amount of money to spend on the many needed improvements and additions. In a sense this is the city's allowance, and it has to be budgeted wisely in order to achieve the greatest benefit. The city planners prepare a Capital Improvements Program, which details every project the city will undertake for the next five years and identifies where the money will come from to pay for each project. This five-year plan is revised every year.

I came to understand how the real problems confronting our cities were social, rather than physical, problems. Physical solutions are only a means to achieving larger social objectives.

I visited the City Planning Commission's library and saw a world of books about architecture, planning, sociology, economics, and engineering. It's really incredible how many fields the city planner has to be familiar with. I learned, to my surprise, that there are Master's and Doctorate programs in many universities to train city planners. Planners often also gravitate from specialized fields, like architecture, law, and economics, into the position of city planner.

Before I left, I browsed through some of the recent reports prepared by the staff, and I took several home with me to read. I also took a copy of the base map for my neighborhood and was very pleased when the planners suggested that I team up with some of my friends to prepare a plan for our own community. They said they would be very interested in the plan we would develop, and I promised to come back and show it to them. I am also planning to attend one of the meetings of the City Planning Commission. I really want to see how they make the decisions using the recommendations prepared by the staff.

For more information about city planning, see the sections "Architect," "Road Building and Repairing," and "Zoning" in this book.

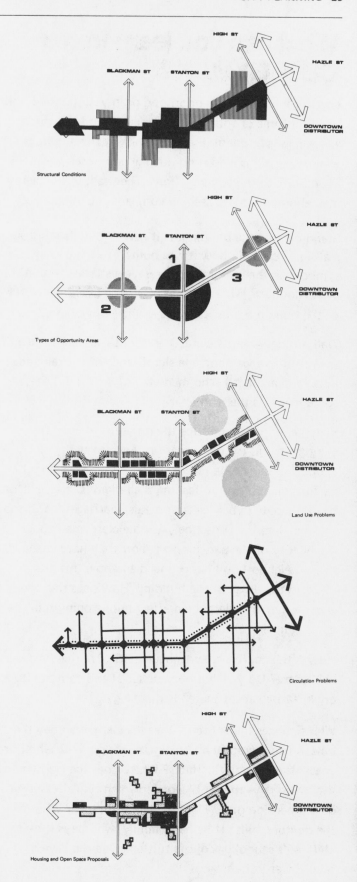

Structural Conditions

Types of Opportunity Areas

Land Use Problems

Circulation Problems

Housing and Open Space Proposals

What can you learn from a CLERGYMAN?

Look around your neighborhood or in your phone book and find three or four different clergymen from different religions or denominations. Look at the buildings where worship is held, find out the day of services, look at and talk to the congregations. Then talk to the clergymen about what you see and compare your findings.

Stand outside the building. Is it new or old? Is there special significance in how it was built? Are there religious symbols on the building—crosses, Jewish stars, stained-glass windows? What do they mean? What is the history of the building? Was it always a house of worship?

Walk inside. Ask the clergyman about the significance of the room arrangement, the significance of the religious items and artifacts. Who made them? Where did they come from? Is there an altar?

Watch a service and notice the different roles of the clergyman and the congregation. Ask the clergyman about the religion he teaches. What other roles does he perform in addition to leading the religious service? Does he participate in baptisms, funerals, marriages, confirmations, or family counseling? Ask the clergyman about the history of the parishioners—how they have changed as the neighborhood has changed and how this has affected the usage of the building. How does this congregation or this clergyman affect public opinion in the community?

How is the church or synagogue used? Are there classes held there? Do youth groups or social and community organizations meet there? Is there a gym?

Who finances the church? Does the clergyman pay the bills, hire a secretary and maintenance people? Who purchases the religious artifacts? Where does the clergyman live? Who pays the rent? Do clergymen retire? Does he have a pension plan? Does he have insurance? Who pays the doctors' bills? If he has a family, who pays for his children's school or college tuition? Does he have a special wardrobe?

In his religion, what is the hierarchy of authority and who makes the higher appointments? Finally, talk to some members of the congregation and the neighborhood and see if they view the role of this church or synagogue in the same way as the clergyman does.

What can you learn from a COMPUTER PROGRAMMER?

Computers have become an important part of our lives, and there are thousands of people employed in the computer field. Of the approximately 125,000 computer programmers, most are working in large business organizations and government agencies. A great many work for insurance companies and banks, public utilities, wholesale and retail establishments, and manufacturing plants of almost every kind. Many programmers employed in government offices do work related to scientific and technical problems or process the vast amount of paperwork. A growing number are employed by computer manufacturers and independent service organizations, which furnish computer and programming services to organizations on a fee basis.

You can find computer programmers in any of the places just listed or in vocational schools or computer training schools. When you enter a large company or a

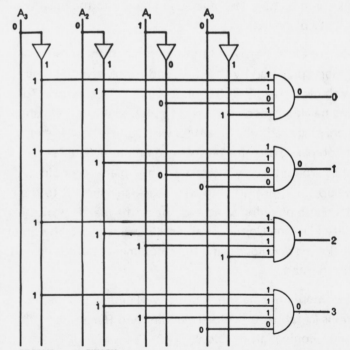

DECIMAL	BINARY			
	A_3	A_2	A_1	A_0
0	0	0	0	0
1	0	0	0	1
2	0	0	1	0
3	0	0	1	1
4	0	1	0	0
5	0	1	0	1
6	0	1	1	0
7	0	1	1	1
8	1	0	0	0
9	1	0	0	1

Conversion of binary to decimal digits is accomplished by this circuit, made up of four not circuits and four and circuits. The truth table at left shows the binary equivalent for the decimal digits from 0 to 9. To show the principle involved in decoding binary digits, the circuit carries the decoding only as far as decimal digit 3. The signal at each of the numbered outputs is 0 unless all the inputs are 1. In the example this is true for the third and circuit from the top, labeled 2. Thus the binary digits 0010 are decoded to yield the decimal digit 2.

service organization, ask for the head of the data processing department. Besides visiting and questioning the programmer, you might also want to talk to data processors, key punchers, computer science instructors, and management personnel who utilize the computer to solve some of their management problems. Here are some questions you might ask about computers:

How do you operate a computer? What are computers used for? What kinds of problems does the computer deal with? Can a computer automatically bill customers? How many different computer systems are there? What is a system? What is a computer language? Who makes it up? How does a programmer know what facts are needed for a specific problem, for example, a customer's bill? Can a computer answer questions we do not have the answers to? What is a flow chart? What is a run? What are terminals? How does a computer read a card or tape? How does the programmer translate the results of the completed program to the individual who wanted the information? What is the difference between the responsibilities of, for instance, the programmer and the data processor?

How large are computers? Does the size of the computer relate to the work that it does? Does each company that wants a computer buy it outright or can you rent them? Are computers only for office use? Are there such things as household computers? If so, what are they used for?

In order to find answers to your questions you might want to visit the manufacturers directly in their factory or sales office (some of the larger ones are IBM, Honeywell, and Burroughs) and question them about their sales. Whom do they sell to? Have the costs risen? Have more computers been sold? In what direction are computers moving? Are more towns and cities using them for such things as traffic control, pollution control, or information storage? Are more hospitals and social agencies using the computer? How has the computer affected our daily lives? What dangers are there in the use of the computer, and are there any checks on misuse?

To round out your view, interview not only those directly involved with the computer—like the programmer—but also doctors who might be experimenting with its use, salesmen, prospective customers, city engineers, department stores (billing departments), and registrars at colleges to see how they use the computer.

What can you learn at a CONSTRUCTION SITE?

I'd seen a hundred construction sites before, just like this one—maybe even a thousand. It was just an ordinary office building like so many others—modern, thirty stories high, and ugly. But since I had to pass it every day, I figured it had to be worth more than the mud and dust and noise as punctuation for my daily walk to school.

It all started very simply. I began to stop for a few minutes each day and look at what was going on. You know, it is really amazing when you realize how many things we never see that have to go into a building to make it work. I always used to wonder how everyone on a large construction site knows what he is supposed to do and when he's supposed to do it. To an untrained eye it all looks like thousands of tiny ants crawling around a piece of forgotten cake.

Then, after a week of gazing from across the street, there were too many things I couldn't understand. I was full of questions. So I began asking workmen: "What's this?" and "What's that do?" — and a hundred other probably stupid questions. But, like most everybody else, they loved talking about what they were doing. I guess they were pleased to feel important—to have someone acknowledge that they knew things that other people didn't. Every day thereafter we used to have little talks—about foundations, girders, riveting, climbing cranes, unions, or any question that happened to pop into my head. I learned about heating and air conditioning, about pouring concrete, about laying bricks, and about lots of other things, too. I used to kid the men about being professors of construction, and I would look forward to each new class. Jim and Ernie and I became good friends.

Once they took me into the construction shack (an entire portable office in an enormous trailer), and they explained how to read the blueprints and how everyone on the construction site knew what he was supposed to do. The blueprints are actually the working drawings prepared by the architects. Every little detail is on them. Because even the construction crew sometimes finds them baffling, Jim and Ernie and the other guys used to refer to them as the "funny papers."

Since photography is one of my hobbies, I began to carry my camera with me and take a picture of the construction site every other day from the same spot. I collected 83 sequential photographs of the progress they were making and mounted them on my wall to form a sort of time-lapse picture of the building being made. It's incredible to look carefully at the pictures and begin to notice which things have appeared since the previous photograph—and to realize how fast some things got done and how long others took. It's a little like cutting down a tree and examining the rings.

The whole experience proved so interesting that I found myself going to the library to find books to add to the things I was learning from the "professors" and to answer the little questions there wasn't time to ask. I had never had so much fun visiting the library before. I guess it's true that you have the most fun learning things you really want to know.

(1) Folded unit in place, showing supporting beams in place (2) Unfolding floor and end wall (3) Unfolding side walls (4) Unfolding roof (5) Completed house

What can you learn standing on the CORNER?

Standing on the corner can mean more than just waiting for the bus or a friend for lunch. Each city street corner, especially in commercial areas, is the scene of increased activity and intensity of vehicles and pedestrians. It is the place where stopping, crossing, turning, waiting, and decision making all occur. No wonder traffic jams happen here. There are so many options: turn right, turn left, go straight, cross, wait, run, stop, meet, buy, look, hop the bus or trolley, ease through the crush of pedestrians as you turn the corner.

Notice whose day-to-day working space the corner is—everyone from sidewalk vendors, panhandlers, newspaper sellers, to foot police, mounted police, meter maids, petitioners, leafleteers, and flower sellers. Over 24 hours the pace and kind of activity of the corner change dramatically. Take a picture from the same point of view every hour for 24 hours to discover just what those changes are in traffic and pedestrian flow, light, artificial light, population. What does the busiest time of the corner have to do with the schedules of the people who move there? When and why is there the most congestion?

Corners are desirable business places (who does not know the "corner store"? Remember bubble gum, cigarettes, and candy?) because of the activity and the number of people who meet and separate there. Find out what businesses are on the corners and if there is any difference in the rent they pay from that of the store next door. How many and what different products, causes, places, and services are advertised and/or displayed at, above, and below eye level? What can you see on foot that you can't see by car, and vice versa?

Where are the accesses and exits to and from other spaces? There are probably subway stairs, doorways, concourse entrances, lobbies, turnstiles, or bus stops. Check the noise level and its sources. Is it different from that of the streets that lead into the intersection?

Compare different corners—commercial, residential, and industrial. Who hangs around them? Is it a social and meeting place? Watch the people for a while. Notice how pedestrians on a busy street move. Speeded up film footage shows how Americans studiously avoid

What can you learn in a COURTROOM?

There are many different kinds of courts. They correspond, first, to the levels of government that legislate the laws that are considered in them. There are city (municipal), state, and federal courts, and each of these is divided into levels corresponding to the appeals process. Often there are also civil and criminal divisions, according to whether a crime has been committed or whether one party is suing another party for damages incurred through some fault not recognized as a crime. In many cities, there are also small claims courts.

You can obtain court schedules, called dockets, wherever the courts are located. You can find their locations in the telephone directory under "Courts" in the section on your city. Most courts are open to the public, and visiting them is a unique experience, since tape record-

physical contact. Movement in fast motion is like a great staccato dance.

Look around at the multiplicity of signs, information, and directions for pedestrians and vehicles, each vying for attention but often lost in the collage. How many different kinds of information are offered there and to whom? How effective do you think it is?

Find out what's under your feet—there is at least a maze of utility lines running under the pavement and macadam. Each utility has its own manhole and an identifying symbol on the cover. How about the subway, sewers, tunnels, concourses, stores, banks, and restaurants? Some of the great railroad stations are underground. Take a good look at the curb and think about why it's there, what it's for and why it is the way it is. Does it do the job it was meant to do? If not, what could? Are you protected on the corner or will you get wet when it rains and maybe splashed? What could be done to eliminate this?

Count cars, trucks, taxis, trolleys, buses, out-of-state license plates. Shop. Buy a paper.

Meet you at the corner.

QUALIFICATIONS TO SERVE AS JUROR TO BE FILLED OUT IN OWN HANDWRITING

Date   Result   By Whom Examined
Do not write in this box

The undersigned certifies to the following answers { Explanations or remarks concerning answers may be made in ruled box on reverse side } :

A person who knowingly makes a false statement of a material fact in these certificates is guilty of a misdemeanor, punishable by fine or imprisonment.

1 Print name in full.. MARY   MARGARET   MURPHY
   First Name   Middle Name   Last Name

2 Date of birth.. 9   12   1936
   Mo.   Day   Year

3 Residence.. 42 .. Street 31ST .. City New York .. Town or Village.. Tel. No. 573-1820

4 How long living at present address 12 years .. How long in N. Y. State 30 yrs .. In County..

5 Give any other name you have used or been known by.. NONE

6 Place of Birth.. Boston .. If not American born, how became citizen.. When naturalized.. Where..
   City   State

7 Education: Primary (High School), College, degrees, special studies, etc...

8 Occupation.. SALESWOMAN .. Employed at present yes .. Business address 5th Ave .. P.O. Zone No.. Tel. No. 382-1074

9 Firm name of employer.. SAKS .. How long in present employment 7 years

10 What other employment during past six years.. None

11 Wife's name.. Her occupation.. Her firm.. Her business address..

12 Do you or your wife own property (such as bank account, furniture, insurance, trust funds, stocks, bonds, mortgages, land, etc.,) worth $250.. yes

13 Ever served as a juror.. no

14 Are you physically disabled or incapacitated.. no .. Is your hearing or eyesight so impaired that you could not intelligently follow a case in court.. no

15 Ever had a motor vehicle license revoked or suspended.. no .. Ever been convicted of a criminal charge.. no

16 If your answer to any question on lines 14 or 15 is "Yes", give all particulars..

17 Any judgments outstanding against you.. no .. Nature of action in which obtained..

18 Have you such views concerning the death penalty as would prevent you from finding a defendant guilty if the crime charged be punishable by death.. no

19 In what months of the year between September 1 and June 30 would you prefer to serve (Name two or more months).. March, June

THE MAKING OF A FALSE STATEMENT OF A MATERIAL FACT IN THIS QUESTIONNAIRE IS A MISDEMEANOR, PUNISHABLE BY FINE AND IMPRISONMENT.

The foregoing answers are true in all respects

Sign here.. Mary Murphy

ers and television or movie cameras are seldom allowed. You can only see the real thing by being there.

While court is in session, there will be no opportunity for asking questions. The process keeps everyone busy and serious. But you may be able to talk to someone after the trial is over. Or, and perhaps better yet, talk to a lawyer, judge, court reporter, or political scientist involved in justice matters before you go to court. That way you will better understand what you're seeing. Not all lawyers try cases in court, but if you can find a trial lawyer, ask when he is next appearing in court and plan to attend.

The courtroom procedure is very standardized, and the roles of the participants are well defined, so you can learn a lot just by observing. How is a jury selected? What are the different roles played by the judge, jury, defense, defendant, prosecution, witnesses? What does it mean when a witness is "under oath"? What is perjury? What are the penalties for perjury? What is a public defender?

What kinds of rules for courtroom behavior can you discover by watching the participants in a trial? How do the people in the courtroom show respect for the judge? When may a witness refuse to answer a question? What kinds of things can a lawyer object to? What is "contempt of court"? If a defendant is found guilty, does he have any recourse other than to accept the verdict? Why do you think that the courtroom procedure is so formal?

There are many technical and procedural aspects to a trial, but once you understand how these work you will come to see how everything is designed in order to guarantee the realization of justice. The judicial process is central to the success of our democratic system. You may see things happen with which you disagree or that will make you angry. Usually, there are good explanations for these occurrences, but you will have to find someone to explain them.

Court reporters, being unbiased parties who spend a great deal of time in courtrooms, would be ideal, if you can find one. These are the men and women who record the verbatim (word for word) transcriptions of the trial on stenotype machines. You will find them listed in the Yellow Pages directory under "Reporters—Court and Convention." While you're asking about the things that happen in a courtroom, get them to show you how their stenotype machines operate—that's fascinating in itself.

What can you learn at a DEPARTMENT STORE?

Any city has at least one department store. That is a store that sells many different items, not specializing in any one thing. Each type of merchandise has a department, or area, in the store where it is sold. Walk down the main street and look for one or check the Yellow Pages under "Department Stores." Depending on what you are interested in finding out about, there are many people who can help you. You can just go in and chat with one of the sales men and women or talk with a floor manager or department head about the organization of his department. Or you can telephone the public relations office and have a chat with someone there about store departments, concessions, pricing, buying, budgeting, billing, credit, consumer protection, printing, and advertising. That's what I did, and I had the nicest, most helpful and informative chat with the head of public relations of one of the largest department stores in Philadelphia.

He explained that there were two types of department stores: those held as private corporations and those owned by the public, that is, those that sell stock to the public. The particular store I was in, Wanamaker's, is privately owned. They have very few concessions in this store; the only one of note is Necchi Sewing Machines, which has only one place of business in each city.

John Wanamaker was the first person in the world to introduce the practice of fair prices, in 1865. This means that a store puts the price of a particular item on a ticket and that price cannot be bartered. Before 1865, all prices in stores could be bartered. The next revolutionary act on the part of Wanamaker's was to institute the idea of a refund: "If it doesn't suit the folks at home, bring it back and we will give you a refund." This policy was announced on January 27, 1866. These two policies were soon copied all over the world.

I asked the public relations director to tell me a little about why people come to this store. They come primarily for four reasons:
1. They have confidence in the merchandise.
2. They have confidence in the advertising.
3. The store is attractive to look at.
4. The store is centrally located.

UP-TO-THE-MINUTE SMART BLAZERS $12.95

The public relations director told me that Wanamaker's is like a self-contained little city. "We hire all our own buyers, who go all over the world to select and buy things for the store. We also have our own importers, and we train our own personnel in all departments. Our store has its own billing and credit department. We have our own restaurants and kitchens. We have our own commercial art department. We offer executive courses for all employees. This allows them to advance if they want and to go into different areas of work. We have a library for our employees, also. We even used to have a track and tennis courts on the roof for the use of our employees."

I asked about different areas of the store. "How do different departments get their goods to sell?"

"Each department is given a certain amount of money to spend each year and told to go out and buy. What they buy they try and sell. Some items sell better than others."

This brought up the question of what happens to goods that just don't sell.

"Well, take, for example, a $5,000 coat. It doesn't sell, so we put it on sale and mark it down to, say, $3,500. It still doesn't sell, so it is marked down even farther to, say, $1,000. It is still on the racks. So then another company comes in, a company whose business is to find these items and buy them up to resell to discount stores, like Filene's Basement in Boston, that deal with merchandise like this."

This example lead me to ask about pricing.

"Our price is determined by the amount of money paid for an item on the wholesale market. Our markup varies from department to department and ranges from 15 percent to 60 percent. We take inventory twice a year to determine what is selling and what is not and to find out in general where we are."

Visit a department store in your city. Talk to the public relations director or a department head and then to some employees. Are their statements and opinions about the store the same? If not, how do they vary? Why do you think they vary? You might also visit a small specialty shop in your area and compare it to a large department store.

What can you learn from a DRY CLEANER?

I went across the street and spoke with the dry cleaner I usually take my clothing to. He was more than willing to tell me about the "process of dry cleaning," as he himself called it. He even provided the questions and then went on to answer them himself.

"Let's take a shirt first. What happens to that? Well, I put it into the laundry right here at the shop. If the customer wants a little or a lot of starch in it, I put that in. When the shirt comes out I have a special machine that presses the collars. They get done first. Then the shirt goes through a steam tunnel and gets dried, pressed, and folded and put into a box. Each of our customers is given a number, and this number is stamped onto the shirt on the inside of the collar so it doesn't get lost.

"Now, what about a woolen dress with two spots on it? First I ask the customer if he can remember what made the spots; are they lipstick or chocolate pudding? I try spot removers. These take about one and a half hours to dry. If this agent does not work, I usually wait until the next day, because it takes so long and I have to watch my time because of the money involved. To dry the dress I look and see what the materials are and then dry it accordingly. My machine for dry cleaning takes 50 pounds for each operation. One operation can last anywhere from 20 to 45 minutes. Most synthetic materials take about 32 minutes."

"What about the big bags I see you taking out of the shop sometimes? What's in those?" I asked.

"That's underwear. Sometimes there's just too much to do here at this shop, and I take it up to my larger plant in the Northeast.

"What about men's suits? You didn't ask me about them. Well, they're done just like the dresses. I check to see if there are any spots. My dry cleaning machines don't use solvents; they use cartridges. They are more expensive, but they don't make the mess the solvents make. You have to change the cartridges once a month. These are solvents, but they come in cartridge form. When we press a suit or dress we have to take into consideration the material it is made of. If it is nylon, we don't press it; we steam dry it.

"Now, what about suede cleaning? Well, that takes 15 minutes extra. I have a new machine at my other plant. I just got it two months ago, and it is just for the cleaning of suede.

"We also do alterations right here at the shop. If the job is too big for us or something we don't do, I take it to two ladies who do work for me outside the shop."

I then asked him about these other shops that appeared to have no machines in them to do dry cleaning.

"They're what we call drop shops. Those places just take in garments to be cleaned. A big pick-up truck comes and takes them to wholesale cleaners where they are cleaned and brought back for pick-up by the customer."

I asked him how he knew so much about chemicals and chemical processes.

"My family has been in the dry cleaning business for I don't know how long. My uncle has a plant and so do my brother-in-law and my father. I should know."

Visit a dry cleaner in your neighborhood. Here are some questions you might ask a dry cleaner: What is the process that the clothes go through after I bring them to you? Ask a definite question: How do I get blackberry juice out of my pink party dress? How long does it take?

Talk to the person who takes your clothes from you or go back and talk to one of the pressers about his work.

Ask him about:

Chemicals and chemistry	Dying and dyes
Profits	Steam and steam cleaning
Charging	Textiles and materials
Bookkeeping	Tailoring
Pollution	Mending
Stains and their removal	Washing
How the machines work	Detergents and soaps

What can you learn from an ELECTRICIAN?

We are so dependent on electricity that without it our sophisticated society would dissolve into a primitive struggle for survival. Food would rot without refrigeration; trains would stop; men would shave with straight razors; and most of us would go to bed at dinner time, since it would be nearly impossible to go out on unlit city streets. Stores could not stay open at night without lights. There would be no movies, no television, no record players. We would freeze in the winter and swelter in the summer. Christmas trees would no longer sparkle with tiny lights.

From time to time electrical appliances fail. And it is only the electrician, who works in the web of wires that runs through every house, every office building, and every factory, who can handle the crises that occur. Of course, the private electrician is different from the electric company, which is a public utility. The electric company is responsible for supplying your whole house or apartment building with electric power. If something goes wrong on their end, you don't have any electricity at all! But if it's a question of a single appliance or a single outlet, an electrician is the person to call. An electrician will come to you, day or night, if your house is suddenly plunged into darkness, your freezer won't freeze, or you've gotten stuck in an elevator. He knows all about fuses, volts, and amperes, and he'll probably explain them to you if you ask. He may have taken an ICS course (International Correspondence School) to learn more about a certain field, or he may be a specialist in airconditioners for large industrial complexes.

Electricians have a bible of the industry called the *National Electrical Code.* The code is forever changing. The 1971 edition, for instance, contained five new chapters and some 400 other changes. Because the field changes so swiftly, an electrician has to be a whiz-kid in business as well as in wiring. He must provide clients with estimates, make out bills, and pay his own taxes and social security, since he's frequently his own boss. He must understand the law so he can read and respond to new legislation that affects his work, such as the Occupational Health and Safety Act, because the men who enforce these acts come around to inspect building sites. They can fine an electrician $70 if he forgets to protect even one electrical cord.

Because electricians all belong to a union, and because their work is so specialized, their prices are high. If there's ever an electrician at work in your school or home, you might as well get your money's worth by learning as much as you can from him. And if you need help with a fuse box, an electric heater, or a toaster, look under "Electricians" in the Yellow Pages.

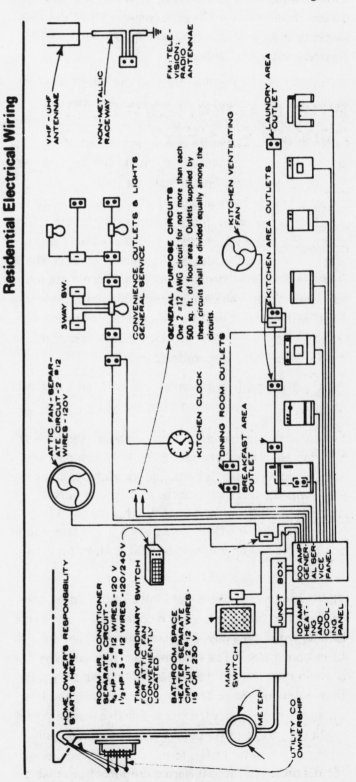

Residential Electrical Wiring

What can you learn at a FOOD DISTRIBUTION CENTER?

The day began with a fifty-minute trip from City Hall to the Food Distribution Center. The way was not marked until I reached Snyder Avenue, where the Food Center had its own bus sign reading: "Route 4 for the Food Distribution Center."

When I arrived and walked through the gates I was amazed at the amount of activity—huge trucks and trailers going in all directions and small pick-ups darting between them. Men were coming in and out of George's Restaurant, and since this led off the building that housed all the stores or stalls for trading, I decided to stop in there and get my bearings and listen to what was going on. Inside, there was quiet talk about who drove which truck, who turned over which truck where, what loads were in which truck and where it was bound, what firms had offered whom more money for what. Other men were getting triple-sized thermoses filled with coffee. I heard a great number of regional accents as extra sides of bacon and a breakfast of meatballs and spaghetti were ordered at 9:30 A.M.

After getting my bearings and listening, I felt I was not quite so noticeable as when I first walked in.

I spoke with a man who, as I learned later, is known as a porter. He is hired at about 6:00 A.M. each day to load trucks. His price is bargained for with the company that owns the truck or with the truck driver himself on instruction from the company. This man said he would probably load only one truck a day. I later found out that his day might begin at 3:00 A.M. and finish at noon.

Then I spoke with the owner of one of the stores, and he explained how the loading is done. "If a truck wants loading, you find a guy, give him your slips, and he loads your truck." The slips are order slips with the company's name and the amount of an item they want to purchase on them. The porter goes around and fills these orders and loads the truck. For this work a porter might get forty to fifty dollars, if he has to load only one product, but if he has to make six or seven stops, that is, get six or seven different products from that many stores, then he might earn sixty or seventy dollars a day.

I was getting up to leave when I thought I saw an empathetic man. I more or less plunked myself down on the other side of his ham, eggs, toast, and hot chocolate and told him generally what I was doing and what I wanted to know from him. His response was, "I'll do what I can. I'll tell you what I know." And with that he began. He took a breath, and it was as though he had been forewarned of my pending arrival, for out came the last ten years of his life.

"I started after the service. I got out in 1960 and got myself a small pick-up. I drove lumber at first. Business was pretty good, so I stayed with lumber and started hauling out of Cleveland. I left lumber and started driving for Shell Oil. I drove an oil tanker, and by that time my kids had started comin' so I drove the school bus, too. My wife, she learned to drive, too. By this time I really wanted to be on my own, so I borrowed money and bought a truck and hauled steel. But then the steel strike came along, and I was forced over into meat. I hauled out of Sioux City, Iowa, to all over the East Coast, but return trips were hard to land, so I changed to Chicago. Hauled LTLs from Chicago to upstate New York—Albany, Schenectady, Utica. That's rough country up there."

Here I interrupted him to find out what LTLs were. They are less than a truck load. He also explained the rates charged for LTLs and truck loads. For example, 1000 pounds to Philadelphia from Chicago costs $3.80 per hundred pounds, 5000 pounds from Chicago costs $2.80 per hundred, and 35,000 pounds, which is a truck load, costs $1.64 per hundred. "I hauled all kinds of meat from twenty different shippers to twenty different wholesalers, everything from meat pies and steaks to frozen bacon to barreled meats and casings. Those are the intestines used for sausage covers.

"I take my kids along sometimes. My son, he's nine, knows how to change oil and check the tires with a hammer. With my wife driving now she sometimes takes a second truck if we have two trucks going to the same place.

"I got one of my six trucks out of Denver now. It's swinging meat to Akron, Ohio." Here I asked about swinging, which means meat swinging on hooks.

"Sometimes pigs are tied instead of hooked, as a hook weighs about four pounds and you got 300 hooks in a truck, well that's a lot of weight just in hooks. Tie 'em up instead, and you can haul another pig."

Here my friend returned to his eating then began talking again about the difficulties of the trucking business.

"Hard to get a load back to Denver. These people in the East, they eat a lot but don't seem to produce enough raw materials to haul back." A long pause followed, while I wrote furiously. The subject then changed to rigs (trucks).

"Guys working for large companies like Spector or Tie, they get a different rig on each trip. They don't care about them. You never see a company truck with chrome. My guys, now, they're different. They take pride in their trucks. Costs are so high, they better."

I asked him how he got in to Philadelphia.

"I loaded Friday night in Chicago and drove home to Akron. I was there Saturday and Sunday. Worked all day Sunday on the trucks and then left Sunday night and got into New York City about seven Monday morning.

"The cream on the top in this business is the return load. I only came to Philadelphia to see a guy about a return load. Now I can't even find him." And with that statement he told me more facts about the expenses of trucking. For example:
1. It costs $28,000 to buy a tractor (cab), $15,000 to buy a trailer with a refrigerator unit, $1300 per year collision insurance, and $1300 per year liability insurance.
2. Cargo insurance varies with what you haul, about $500 to $1500 a year and up.
3. Liability on the trailer is 10 percent of the insurance rate on the tractor.
4. The cost of a license plate is about $1100 a year, but this also varies depending on where you are initially licensed. In Wisconsin it costs $1100 a year, and in Illinois, $1300 a year. In Ohio it costs $350, but in that state you must buy prorated plates for other states. Some states have reciprocal agreements; in others you must pay to pass through.

My friend also told me that each state has a fuel tax. Take Pennsylvania, for example. Pennsylvania has 350 miles of turnpike, which is the usual way to cross the state. An average truck gets 3.5 miles to the gallon, so

the truck should buy 100 gallons in Pennsylvania and pay state tax on that 100 gallons. But if you only buy 50 gallons in the state you are still responsible for the tax on the 50 gallons you didn't buy. This cost is averaged out quarterly, not on each trip. The fuel department of each company does this work.

"A large company will have a fuel tax department and a licensing department. New York and Ohio have a road tax, but Ohio has no fuel tax. Ohio's road tax is equal to 2 cents a mile on a five-axle truck, which is levied on every road but the turnpike. New York has both a road and a fuel tax.

"Every trip has a manifest. This is a statement that tells what is being hauled where and at what weight, how many miles the truck is going, and how many miles through each state. Each state has the right to inspect this manifest. The Western states often poke a stick in the fuel tank to check for gas taxes. Most states have weighing stations along the roads that do spot checking on weights and manifests to make sure that they correspond. Some of the Western states even have definite ports of entry that truckers must pass through to enter the state.

"You put all you can get on a truck usually. This is the rule on good-paying freight. I wouldn't overload on truck-load-rate freight, though. LTLs pay double or triple in prices to what a truck load pays. There are times when the trucking industry wants you to haul 40,000 pounds and you can only haul 39,000 pounds legally, so there you are, overloading. You can get by with 500 pounds.

"I think the load should depend on two things: braking power and horsepower; some kind of ratio should be worked out. Some trucks with 220 horsepower and a flimsy trailer are allowed to haul 47,280 pounds. This is figured out on the basis of, say, that truck I just spoke of with 220 horsepower. His light weight (unloaded) is, say, 26,000 pounds. The legal limit in most East Coast states is 73,280 pounds, so that amount minus 26,000 gives this flimsy truck a possible load of 47,280. Now I come along with 350 horsepower and a good trailer and light weight at 33,000 pounds, which leaves me 43,000 to load. Yet the other guy is climbing hills at 20 miles per hour. I can go 40 or 50 miles per hour. Who is safer? Why shouldn't I be able to haul 47,000? These weight laws vary greatly among states. Ohio allows 78,000 pounds, but most of the East

Coast allows 73,280. Speed limits vary, too: 70 miles per hour in Colorado, 65 in Nebraska, same as cars in Indiana, 65 in Michigan, 65 on the New York Thruway. All these things should be regulated—the speeds and weights, fuel taxes, road taxes, and license plate costs.

"There's also a Federal Highway Use Tax. This is also regulated according to type of vehicle and weight. This varies anywhere from $180 to $250 a year."

Then the truck driver had to go find the man about a load to haul to Denver. On top of all his concerns was the recent news that this morning one of his six trucks turned over outside Chicago. The driver was unhurt. My friend said good-bye.

I wandered out of the restaurant and up the aisle between the rears of the open trucks waiting for the porters to fill them and the stores or stalls that displayed their clean, fresh produce to buyers and lookers who strolled the walkway. I spoke with one man who had worked at his job as manager for only two years. Before he began, he had never thought of this type of work, but now he couldn't be budged. "I wouldn't be in anything else: good men to work with, interesting things going on all the time."

I went on and came to a store that had a crate of small, hard green things that I didn't immediately recognize. "They're raw olives," someone said.

"And what can I do with them?" I asked.

"Crack them with a wooden mallet, then soak them in salt brine or, some people, they like to soak them in lye to take the bitterness out. Soak them for three months. Garnish them with celery, parsley, and oregano to suit your own taste. You know, experience is the best teacher. Then they're ready to eat."

I thanked him for the recipe that he had imparted so warmly, and I felt that it was kind of indicative of the feeling of the whole market: people obliging and warm and showing a sense of enjoyment in their work. Maybe it was the sense that comes from knowing that they are feeding the millions of the city. (It may sound corny, but it really is there.)

What can you learn from a GARBAGE MAN?

The following information was gathered from a private garbage collector and from a man in the City Sanitation Department (see the section "City Hall"), Mr. Watson, who was most eager to talk.

Official definition of *garbage:* What remains after preparation or consumption of food. The word *trash* applies to everything else.

Garbage

Garbage is collected by private firms or private collectors, such as farmers. They get these jobs from open competitive bidding. Private collection is responsible for 90 percent of the garbage collection. Household garbage is collected twice a week. Farmers who want this garbage for hog feed collect it directly themselves. There is no middleman.

Trash

Trash is collected once a week. All trash collectors are city employees and therefore civil servants. They must take a Civil Service exam, and their pay scale is determined by length of service. There are two kinds of trash men: the lifters and the drivers. The lifters do the lifting and dumping of cans into the truck. If your institution or place of business requires trash service more frequently than once a week, you must hire your own private trash collector. City trash removers will not collect from manufacturers or from wholesalers.

There are four different sizes of trash trucks—9 cubic yards, 10 cubic yards, 16 cubic yards, and 20 cubic yards. They are all of the compactor type. These trucks take only stuff that can be compacted. The same day as the trash collection, an open truck follows the trash truck in exactly the same route and picks up all the large junk, like refrigerators, beds, and stoves.

Each city-employed trash man works eight hours a day. The trash trucks are kept at six different locations (in the city of Philadelphia). Their maintenance is done by city employees at these locations.

Incineration

There are six incinerators in Philadelphia. Trash is also unloaded at two land-fill areas, and there will soon be a third (for Philadelphia). The incinerators are the worst pollution offenders in the city. This problem is immense because of its complexity. All refuse is burned and therefore gives off all sorts of gases that might individually be controlled. The only products that are salvaged are the metals. These are collected under contract. Cost is the prohibitive factor in sorting the refuse. The Department of Sanitation thought that a partial solution would be to fill up the abandoned strip mines. This alternative was not given the go-ahead because of political pressure. When the present land-fill areas are filled, the trucks will move on until the entire earth has a stratum of garbage encasing its girth.

What plans does your community have for coping with its ever-increasing wastes?

WASTE GENERATION AND DISPOSITION

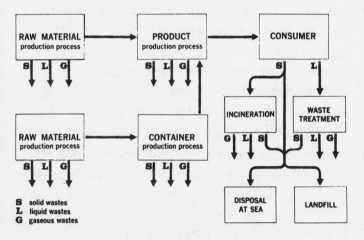

S   solid wastes
L   liquid wastes
G   gaseous wastes

What can you learn at a GAS STATION?

If your car breaks down and requires a full day to repair and you can't make a move without it, perhaps you will be able to pass the time with a gregarious gas station owner. Otherwise, ask a few questions each time you stop in to get gas.

The process behind the gas that goes into your car is fascinating. The gas goes from the field to the ship, to the refinery, and then into the truck that delivers it to the individual gas station. The trucks traveling on the highway usually carry 8,000 gallons to a station with six pumps. The tanks to keep these pumps in operation hold over 4,000 to 6,000 gallons apiece and are under the area you drive over.

The gas station operator makes a profit of from three to six cents a gallon. He pays a wholesale price of about $2,800 for 8,000 gallons. Can you figure out how much he has to sell to pay for it? How is his price for

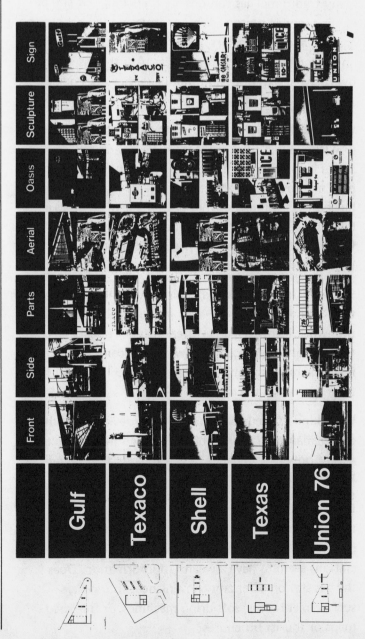

gas set and how many gallons does he sell a year?

Ask the gas station owner his opinion about the performance qualities of the no-lead and low-lead gasolines developed to eliminate air pollution. What percentage of his customers request them? Does he worry about the possibility of electric cars replacing gasoline-driven engines?

If his station is an official inspection station, what requirements about tools and equipment has the state set up for him? Ask him about the test on mechanics that anyone issuing an inspection sticker must pass. The standard rate charged for an inspection sticker is $5.00; the sticker costs 15 cents from the state. Ask him how many cars he inspects each year. How much money does he make from this part of his business?

Many traditional gas stations are branching out and becoming service centers. Where formerly they handled only gas, oil, and light repairs, they now offer tires, batteries, and complete servicing for the car. Ask the gas station owner what extent of automobile service he provides. Does he plan to expand his services?

What are the most prevalent auto troubles he encounters? How much truth is there in stories about high prices being charged for repairs even though the garage may not have discovered the problem? Ask him how he charges for repairs. What percentage of an average bill represents labor? Where does he buy his parts? How does he decide which parts to keep in stock? What is his markup on parts?

Some of the large gas companies have schools where they train individuals to work in the stations. Gas station work involves many different types of cars, in contrast to service garage work, which concentrates on handling only that make of car for which the manufacturer has set up the garage.

What kind of security precautions or devices does the owner maintain? Have robberies forced the station to accept only exact change or credit cards after certain hours at night?

Did you notice during the time you spent there that many people stopped to inquire about hotels, restaurants, road conditions, routes, and homes for sale? Gas stations seem to have a wealth of information. Does the gas station offer any conveniences to travelers—such as rest rooms, soft drink machines, or free road maps or tourist brochures?

What can you learn at a GREENHOUSE?

John works at one of the largest wholesale nurseries in the area. Like many other "plant people" I've met (gardeners, florists, plant lovers, landscape architects, horticulturists, plant store owners), he loves to talk about his business and about plants. "There's something about this work," he said, "that makes you glad to be alive. I've watched this fern over here since it was a baby and now look at it." He gestured toward the enormous staghorn fern that loomed above us. As we walked through the more than fifteen greenhouses, John pointed out to me hundreds of plants at different stages of development, from newly-seeded flats, seedlings, and tiny freshly-potted plants to fully-grown and growing specimens. He explained that this nursery supplied many of the retail plant shops and nurseries in the area and that many plants we were now seeing would be gone in a couple of hours. He reminded me to look all around myself—overhead, where greenery of every description, grape ivy, asparagus ferns, spider plants, and pick-a-back plants, spilled over from hanging baskets,

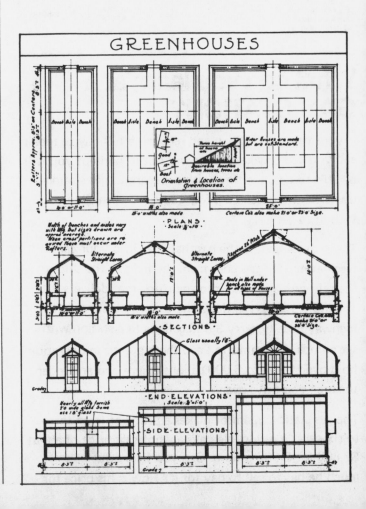
GREENHOUSES

and underfoot, where baby tears and wandering jew nearly carpeted the floor under the plant tables, which were covered with African violets or philodendrons or bromeliads. I could see and feel the nursery's attempt to duplicate the natural habitat and environment of the plants as John pointed out that humidity, temperature, light, water, and food are all carefully regulated. The ferns must be kept out of the sun and fairly wet; the laurel tree needs daily misting, but its roots must be kept fairly dry; the gardenia is just plain temperamental. Each greenhouse we entered nearly took my breath away. Everywhere I looked I saw lush green of every hue . . . row after row, thousands of plants in all.

I could see how complicated it is to manage a nursery like this. Ordering from as far away as California and Florida, importing, transporting, advertising, care and maintenance of the plants, and upkeep of the greenhouses and their equipment keep about 100 employees busy. Some were working on filling orders, invoices, billing and bookkeeping, others were making up fancy combination displays for florists, pruning, watering, wrapping, and packaging. Still others were potting and repotting, seeding, loading moving-van-type trucks, mixing soil. Fighting mites, mealybugs, scale, and other plant pests and diseases is extremely important, too, John said. If the soil gets a white crust on it or if the leaves turn yellow and start to drop, it can mean that the plant is anemic and needs iron. Burying a nail in the soil or adding acid can cure it before the damage is too severe. As we walked along John gave me many other bits of advice on plant care and mentioned Latin and common names of plants I'd never heard before.

In several places I saw hundreds of pots in all sizes and styles of clay, ceramic, and plastic. Room-sized bins near the shipping area overflowed with mounds of soil ready for mixing, and at counters nearby people were potting and repotting plants. John reminded me that the makeup of the soil and the manner of potting have a lot to do with keeping plants healthy.

As we neared the point where we had started our tour, I realized that what had seemed like twenty minutes had been an hour and a half of looking, listening, and asking questions. John invited me to come back again and added, "Doesn't matter what you do. . . . There's just something about growing things and the feel of dirt." I can really understand now what he means.

What can you learn at a HARDWARE STORE?

A hardware store is a gadget-lover's heaven. Nowhere else can you find so many different gadgets in so many different shapes and sizes designed to facilitate almost every kind of mechanical operation. Sometimes you can think up whole projects to work on just by looking at all the items in a hardware store.

There are different kinds of hardware stores. First, there are both retail and wholesale stores. Also, the stock is very different from one to another. Hardware stores may sell any or all of the following:

Paint
Housewares
Keys and locks
Builder's supplies
Glass
Plumbing tools
Building tools
Electrical supplies
Window shades
Floor covering
Appliances
Mill supplies
Storm doors and windows

Garden supplies
Roofing supplies
Snow removal equipment
Decorative hardware for home or office
Automotive supplies
Pet supplies
Toys
Unpainted furniture
Railings
Bathroom supplies
Bolts, nuts, and screws

The kind of hardware store you look for will depend on what you want to know. The easiest place to begin, of course, is the Yellow Pages.

No matter what items the store sells, the owner or manager can tell you about hiring and firing, purchasing, record keeping, salesmanship, understanding and dealing with customers, advertising, and accounting. A hardware store is a good place to learn about all aspects of operating a small business. Through the owner or manager, you can meet the salesmen who sell to the hardware store, the designers from the companies who make up and produce the displays, the tax assessor from City Hall who evaluates the property, the real estate man who rents the property to the owner, or the accountant who prepares the tax records for the owner.

It is interesting to find out why one hardware store carries certain items and why others sell other products. How does the owner determine which products he will sell? How does he decide when to limit the choice of items? How does he decide to carry certain brands of one item, like paint, and when to add a competitor? How are prices determined? How much profit does a store make? What expenses does the hardware store have? What is its overhead? If possible, compare the hardware store with a hardware department of a large department store in terms of stock, costs, and profits.

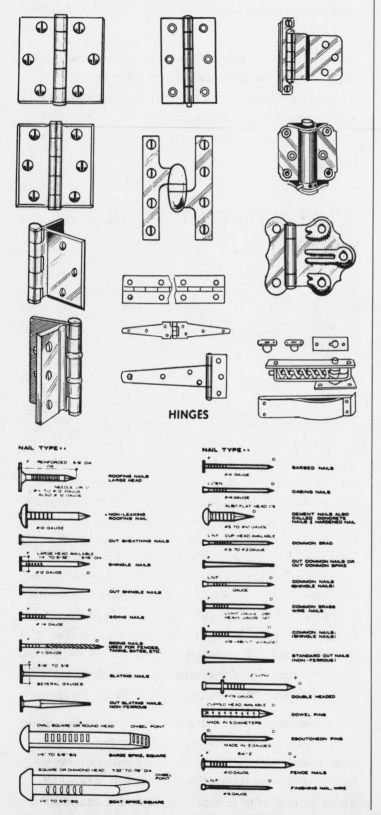

HINGES

What can you learn about a HELICOPTER?

The boy had an urge to fly in a helicopter so with money in pocket, he went to the airport where the rent-a-copter firm was located.

The lowest charge was $95 per hour.

Expediently, he befriended a helicopter pilot who at least allowed him to sit in a whirlybird while they talked. What the pilot told him was almost as exciting as the ride would have been:

"Hours-old babies who are premature or otherwise in danger of permanent health damage are now initiated into our supermodern world with a flight to a hospital's intensive care nursery. Increasingly, new high-rise buildings in many cities are equipped with a helipad on the roof. And passengers flying into airports can hop a helicopter and be taken right into town without losing time traveling on crowded highways.

"Cops and copters have linked up in a program called Sky Knight, which involves patrolling Lakewood, California, by air. Many merchants participate in the program, installing alarm lights on roofs, which are visible to the helicopter for three to four miles in daylight and at greater distances in darkness. In the first year of the project, major crimes dropped by 8 percent."

The boy asked about the origins of the first commercial helicopter.

"A handful of pioneers began using the whirlybird in agricultural flying in 1947," the pilot told him. "By 1960, 936 helicopters were in the skies of the United States and Canada. By 1971, their total had soared to 3,874. Nonetheless, helicopters will not be parked in everyone's driveway, for they are tough to handle and tough to maintain and are expected to remain in the worlds of business and government."

"Have we learned anything as a result of the massive use of helicopters in Korea and Vietnam?" the boy wondered aloud.

"Yes," the pilot replied. "Successful evacuation of battlefield casualties during those wars prompted the use of helicopters for removing the injured from highway accidents and as a replacement for ground ambulances. Today about 275 hospitals in the United States have helistops."

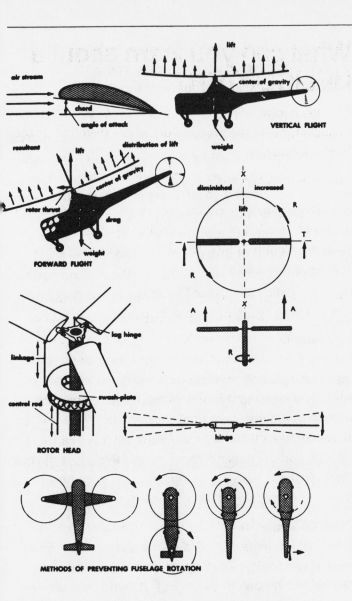

air stream

chord

angle of attack

resultant

lift

center of gravity

VERTICAL FLIGHT

weight

distribution of lift

lift

center of gravity

rotor thrust

drag

weight

FORWARD FLIGHT

diminished

increased

lift

ROTOR HEAD

leg hinge

linkage

control rod

swash-plate

hinge

METHODS OF PREVENTING FUSELAGE ROTATION

"What are some other uses?" the boy asked.

"Certainly you are aware of the airborne traffic reporters who describe traffic conditions to motorists," the pilot mentioned. "And the use of whirlybirds in construction work is also growing—for hauling materials to construction sites or to building tops, for example. Around Christmas some helicopters are hired to transport Christmas trees to building tops. Also, at Christmas some thoroughly modern Santa Clauses arrive by helicopter in the parking lots of suburban stores."

"Suppose I want to take lessons," said the boy.

"Typical costs in the Northeastern states run from $50 to $70 on up to $100 an hour depending on craft size," the pilot reported. "And that fee continues for a minimum of 40 flying hours.

"Incidentally," he told the boy, "it was a woman who made the first solo helicopter flight cross country from California to southern New Jersey."

"What if I get several friends to share the rental cost of $95 an hour?" The boy started to figure.

"Forget it," was the advice. "Around the Northeast that's the rental for a bubble top Bell 47G, which accommodates two passengers and the pilot. The larger J model holds three passengers and a pilot and rents for $135 an hour. Top rental is for a jet-powered Bell Jet Ranger carrying four passengers and a pilot at $200 an hour.

"Why don't you contact the Vertical Lift Aircraft Council of the Aerospace Industries of America, 1725 De Sales Street N. W., Washington, D. C 20036. In addition to having a lot of information on helicopters, pilots, and usage, they may know someone who gives free rides to boys and girls!"

What can you learn at a HOSPITAL?

Inside the walls of any large hospital you will find miniatures of a dozen different kinds of businesses operating in the outside world. Many hospitals are so self-sufficient that if a blackout occurs, as happened along the Eastern Seaboard in 1966, they are even capable of generating their own electricity.

As in any business, the problems of meeting expenses and collecting money exist. Like a hotel, the hospital is concerned with room and board, but these problems are on a much larger and more crucial scale. Housekeeping and laundry, which may seem to be casual maintenance jobs in the outside world, are vital to an institution that requires sterile conditions.

Hospitals vary. Some are proprietary hospitals owned by a group of doctors. Most hospitals are voluntary to some degree, which means that they take in a percentage of poor patients. Others are municipal, caring mainly for indigents, though Medicare may be having an effect on those hospitals. Veterans Administration hospitals, which treat men and women with service-connected problems, make up the balance.

Aside from proprietary hospitals, most hospitals are nonprofit institutions and welcome volunteers. Volunteer work provides an invaluable opportunity to receive firsthand information on the mechanics of a hospital. These jobs include working as a Candy Striper on the hospital floors (delivering mail, flowers, and supplies), or working in the coffee shop or gift shop. Pediatric wards need help entertaining children with stories and games. For more information on what kinds of volunteer jobs a hospital has, check with the personnel department or the public relations department.

Whether you are a volunteer, an observer, a patient, or a visitor, there are many things to learn at a hospital. Here is a list of some of the departments of a hospital, the kinds of people who work in them and what they do, and the things they can tell you about running a hospital.

Dietary Department

This department employs nutrition experts, chefs, and bakers. Try to visit this department at some time other than meal time—perhaps in the early afternoon. These people can tell you how a patient's condition determines what he can eat and why a patient about to undergo an operation can only eat certain things. Ask them what kind of dishes and utensils they use, how they keep food hot, and how they distribute the food throughout such a large building. How do they store large amounts of food? What kind of refrigeration is there? Do they use special cleaning agents in the kitchen?

Admissions Office

People in this office type, answer the phone, make calls, file, design and fill out forms, send out mail, and prepare identification bracelets for patients. Ask them how they keep the hospital operating at maximum capacity. How do they keep track of a patient's location in the hospital? What are the rules about visitors? Have they noticed any trends or patterns in admissions?

Housekeeping and Laundry Services

What kinds of equipment are used for these services? How often are hospital rooms cleaned? How often is linen changed? How much of the linen used is disposable? How is a room kept sterile?

Control Supply Service

The person in this department will probably have a background in pharmacology and possibly in inventory control, also. Here are some questions you might ask: How do you store drugs with specific life spans? How long will something remain sterile? How do you package drugs? What effect does temperature have on drugs? How do you distribute drugs? What are the different units of dosage? What kinds of security are maintained to make sure that drugs are not stolen or misused? How do you decide which drugs to stock, and what kinds of records do you keep of your inventory?

Operating Room

The operating room is one of the most important parts of any hospital. It must be kept sterile at all times, and if you are allowed to see it, you will probably have to wear a sterile cap and gown. Some hospitals will let you observe an operation from behind a glass partition. This is one of the ways that medical students learn about surgery. What kinds of instruments are used? How is a patient put to sleep? How is the heartbeat monitored? How is bleeding controlled? What is done with an organ that has been removed from the body?

Laboratories

There are many kinds of laboratories, each one a highly specialized part of the hospital. Find out what the differences are among the clinical, microbiology, pathology, hematology, cytology, and chemistry labs. What is a diagnostic test? What is a specimen? What is a culture? How do you use a microscope? What other kinds of equipment are used? Visit the blood bank and learn how blood is broken down, stored, typed, tested, and transfused.

Other Departments

Other departments of a hospital include the medical records department, radiology (see the section entitled "X-ray Technician" in this book), radiation therapy, rehabilitation services (see "Social Worker" in this book), and a building and maintenance crew. A hospital also relies on the individual skills of doctors, nurses, computer programmers, statisticians, engineers, and architects. What does each of these people contribute to the operation of the hospital? How does their affiliation with the hospital make their work different from that of others in their field?

What can you learn at a HOTEL?

Almost every town or city has at least one hotel or motel. These can be found in the urban areas or on the outskirts of cities, along major highways. Summer camps, spas, dude ranches, and other related institutions may employ similar people and have similar problems.

The hotel business is complex and requires specialized personnel to conduct daily operations, which may involve thousands of guests yearly. There are different kinds of hotels, and each one has a slightly different operation. The three basic types are commercial, residential, and resort.

Commercial: The majority of hotels fall into this category. These are primarily for transients—travelers who need a room for a short stay.

Residential: These are for people who stay for several months to several years.

Resort: These hotels are primarily for vacationers and are often open only at certain times of the year.

More than 800,000 people are employed in hotels and related businesses. The number of employees in any hotel depends on the size of the establishment. The size of the hotel generally ranges from 25 rooms to as many as 1,000 rooms. Motor hotels also range from the very large to the owner-operated ones, which employ very few, if any, paid workers.

Most large hotels and some motels also have restaurants or coffee shops and employ a full restaurant staff. There are often also banquet facilities, meeting rooms, exhibit halls, and recreational facilities, such as swimming pools, ice skating rinks, movies, golf courses, tennis courts, ski slopes, and sauna baths. There are also barber shops, gift shops, florists, ticket agencies, baby-sitting services, valets, laundry service, newsstands, sightseeing information, and, perhaps, a hotel reservation service for your next stop.

The variety of people who might work in a hotel and whom you might watch and talk to include:

Housekeeping personnel: maids, porters, housemen, linen room attendants, executive housekeepers

Uniformed staff: bellmen, doormen, elevator operators

Front office staff: room clerks, key clerks, mail clerks, information clerks

Clerical staff: bookkeeper, cashier, telephone operator, secretary, reservationist

Management: hotel manager, assistants, food service managers

Restaurant staff: See the section entitled "Restaurant" in this book.

What are their jobs?

There is also another group of employees who may be found elsewhere as well. They include lawyers, accountants, maintenance workers (carpenters, plumbers, electricians, heating and ventilation engineers), chefs, personnel workers, valets, launderers and dry cleaners, florists, barbers, gardeners, beauty salon operators, and detectives.

What do they do?

The best person to introduce you to the hotel is the hotel manager or his assistant. Before you talk with either of them, sit in the lobby and watch the activity. Who carries in the guests' bags? Where do the guests go, what does the room clerk do, why do guests sign in, and who takes the guests to their rooms? What else is happening in the lobby? Is the lobby made for relaxing? Are people in a barber shop, buying postcards, choosing a floral bouquet? What arrangements do these places have with the hotel? Do they rent space? Do they pay the hotel a portion of their profits?

How does a hotel establish room rates? Are they controlled in any way? Is the hotel part of a chain? What are the consequences of being part of a large chain? Must the furniture be the same, or the menu in the restaurant, or the color scheme? Is this kind of arrangement more profitable than an individually owned hotel?

Are there some seasons of the year or certain days of the week that are busier? Does the hotel try to book convention groups or certain kinds of tourists? How is this done? What kind of advertising is done? Who decides credit policy? What happens if someone can't pay his bill?

Hotels, particularly the commercial and resort ones, are constantly dealing with new customers. The hotel can introduce you to almost every aspect of business and customer relations.

What can you learn at an INSURANCE COMPANY?

Here is a list of the different departments that make up an insurance company and the kinds of concepts and skills you can learn about in each one.

Mortgages and Securities
Stocks and bonds
Economics
The market
Public relations
Maintaining contacts
Problem solving
Appraising land and property
Understanding locations and population
Finance
Analyzing a good or bad risk
Being aware of the environment when considering progress and expansion

Personnel
Interviewing
Operation and maintenance of audiovisual equipment (including closed-circuit television)
Teaching
Effective letter writing
Training seminars
Research
Payroll system

General Services
Carpenters
Electricians
Printers
Plumbers
Heating and ventilation engineers
Interior designers
Space planners
Painters
Selection and purchasing of furniture
Inventory control

Art Department
Photography
Writers
Layout
Type selection
Proofreading
Purchasing

Public relations
Marketing

Clerical
Transcription
Word processing
Power typing
Switchboard operation
Packaging
Stamping

Actuarial Department
Determination of rates
Reading and making tables
Understanding graphs
Mathematics
Research

Records Department
Training
Making and following mailing lists
Sales promotion
Test giving, grading, and analysis
Internal and external auditing
Data processing
Computer programming
Keypunch
Microfilm
Filing
Cataloging

Legal Department
Research
Understanding and manipulating taxes

Community Service
Tutoring
Legal help
Financial assistance

Medical
Doctors
Nurses
Lab technicians
Analysis of tests
Interpretation of x-rays
Distribution and dispensation of drugs
Analysis of diseases and medicines

Underwriting
Determination of rates
Logical problem solving

What can you learn from a JOURNALIST?

You've probably seen a journalist—at a baseball game, at a movie opening, at the theater, at the scene of a fire, at a parade, trailing behind politicians, movie stars, and athletes, or at a public demonstration.

A journalist is a question machine. Like most people, he's curious. Unlike most people, he knows how to ask questions that probe and pull for the most complete answers. He might work for a newspaper and be called a columnist. He might just follow his nose, writing about anything that interests him and selling his articles to publishers. Then he'd be called a free-lance writer. You can see him on television news shows, hear him on the radio, or read his column in the paper. If you work for a school newspaper or an office publication (called a house organ), you're a journalist, too.

If you want to be a better one, or if you just want to find out what journalism is all about, walk into the news room at a local television studio, or look at newspapers and local magazines to get their addresses. Since journalists live in a world of words,

you can be pretty sure that they'll enjoy talking. And since they spend all of their time talking and writing about other people, they'll probably be delighted to talk about themselves for a change.

The first thing a journalist will mention is the five Ws: Who, What, Where, When, Why. Answers to the five Ws can usually be found in the first paragraph of any newspaper story. Read a few and find them.

I decided that a good place to find a journalist would be at a newspaper plant. (To learn more about newspaper publication, see "Newspaper Plant" in this book.) When I got to the plant, I was surprised at how open and barren and noisy the working area was. There were really no offices to speak of; the large area was cluttered with desks and machines, and I found it amazing that people could work with no privacy and with so much noise. When I saw the presses, I understood why the building had been designed this way. The presses are so big that they require great amounts of floor space, and the people just have to arrange themselves according to the needs of these machines.

I decided to visit the room where feature stories are written, though I could have gone to the sports department, the business room, the art room, or the print shop.

The journalist I met there introduced herself as Harriet. She talked very fast and seemed to be forever shuffling through the stacks of papers on her desk. She said that when you're a journalist you deal in lots of areas: collecting information, analyzing data, sifting out facts and opinions, researching, reading, dictating, and questioning. She talked about how important it is to be at the right place at the right time and how she spends much of her time traveling around, writing in between appointments.

I learned, while telephones rang and people dashed through the room, about the countless people she meets and works with, about the importance of being accurate, and about the ever-present pressure of deadlines. Ready or not, the newspaper goes to press twice a day. It doesn't wait for a reporter to finish an assignment.

Try following a journalist around for a day or even a few hours. Watch how he locates important people and events. How does he decide what is newsworthy and what isn't? How do people react to his questioning?

What can you learn at a JUNK YARD?

The interesting thing about a junk yard is that someone has made a business out of what other people have thrown away. Junk dealers are listed in the Yellow Pages, and although not all of them work out of a large junk yard, you can call a few and find one who does.

When you arrive at the junk yard, walk into the main office. If you are too shy to start a conversation with the dealer there, just stand around until someone else does. This happens often. Perhaps a truck with wastes will drive in and park on the scale, or someone might stop in to buy a used 1956 Pontiac hood to make a boat. As a rule, junk yards are very busy places.

If you happen to hit the junk yard on a slow day, just set out for yourself among the piles. It's fun to see what other people throw away. What kind of junk do you find? Is everything pretty well beaten up, or are some things in fairly good condition? Do you see anything you yourself could use? How are prices for these discarded items determined? What happens to junk that nobody wants? How much of junk material can be recycled and used again in industry? What kinds of vehicles and machines do you see at the junk yard? How are they used?

One of the more unusual uses of junk is in sculpture and painting. Visit a museum of modern art and see if you can find any traces of junk in the sculpture and painting displayed there.

What can you learn in a KINDERGARTEN ROOM?

The kindergarten room offers the observer an excellent chance to watch young children grow emotionally and physically, adjust to a larger social group, and learn to understand the world in which they live. You can watch the effects of the structure of a room, the effects of the teacher, and the effects of the classroom situation on the child facing a new experience. You can find a kindergarten—public or private—through your local school board or by looking in the telephone directory under your city or town school system. Call the school principal and ask to set up a time for observation.

Watch the children and what they do. Who are these children and what do you look for? The children are generally four or five years old. At four they are constantly active, jumping, running, climbing. They are constantly doing. They are highly egocentric, wanting everyone to watch only them. They do not play in groups. Although they may play near other children, they are really playing alone. They generally do not understand the concept of sharing. They are extremely curious and demand answers. But long explanations will make them impatient, and they are onto new questions long before you have finished answering their original one. They are experimenters and explorers and are constantly looking for support and reinforcement.

As the child moves to his fifth birthday and then toward his sixth, he becomes more cooperative and better able to work in groups; he becomes more independent, his play becomes more organized and more purposeful, and he talks incessantly. However, he retains the need to please and the inability to concentrate for long periods of time.

Watch the children over a period of time; for example, observe a morning session once a week over a semester's time. Make a list of the children's names and mark their progress and the changes in them as the time passes. See if you can guess the age of a child by his behavior.

How long does the child remain with one activity? When does the child say, "Watch me! Watch me!"? Does he play alone? Does he take toys away from others? What makes the child laugh? How does a child get to know an object? Must he touch and feel and push and shove? Does he like to manipulate materials—to pile blocks and sand, to smear finger paint? When does the child do things for himself, like zipping his own snowsuit? How do the children make up games? When do they begin to imitate real-life situations, like playing out their home life or being the bus driver? When do they become more dexterous with their fingers and hands?

How does the child demand attention? How do his demands change as he becomes older? How does he show anger, satisfaction? Is he moody or even-tempered? What are the similarities among the children, and what are the differences?

Watch the things the children work with. These might include:

Musical instruments	Dolls and doll houses
Song books	Household items
Story books	Balls, bats, and ropes
Coloring books	Dress-up clothes
Building blocks	Plants
Animals	Toys and puzzles
Scissors and paper	Films
Paint and crayons	Clay
Blackboards and chalk	Wood and tools

The list of materials is endless. What is important is to watch how the children make use of the materials and how they learn, as they grow, to work with each item and to be more creative and more purposeful in their activities.

Watch the teacher—how she moves about the room, the tone of her voice, the kind of vocabulary, the pace of her actions and words, and the effect of all these things on the child. Also, be sensitive to the children's reaction to you, for your presence, like that of any older person, will be realized, and you will probably be imitated. To get into the kindergarten room over a period of time, you might want to offer your services as a classroom aide.

Watch the room and how it changes. Is the room pleasant, warm, and comfortable? Is the room colorful and alive? Is space utilized well so that there is easy movement? Are materials arranged in such a way as to stimulate the children? Do children move naturally around the room, forming spontaneous groups? How does the arrangement of the room affect the ongoing activities? How does the room arrangement reflect or impose upon the role of the teacher?

How does the room change when the activities change—

for music and singing, for the library, for milk and cookies, for the nap? Is there an area for children's boots and coats? Does each child have his own desk or are there tables? Is there an area for plants to grow, or one for live animals—like rabbits, hamsters, or fish—to live in?

What is the lighting like? Are there movable easels and areas for building blocks? Are there display boards with large pictures or the works of the children affixed to them? Are there numbers and letters around?

Do you think this kindergarten room is well set up to encourage growth and learning on the part of the children? If not, how would you change it? Perhaps the teacher would be interested in your suggestions, if you present them tactfully and in a way that does not discount her own training and experience in the field.

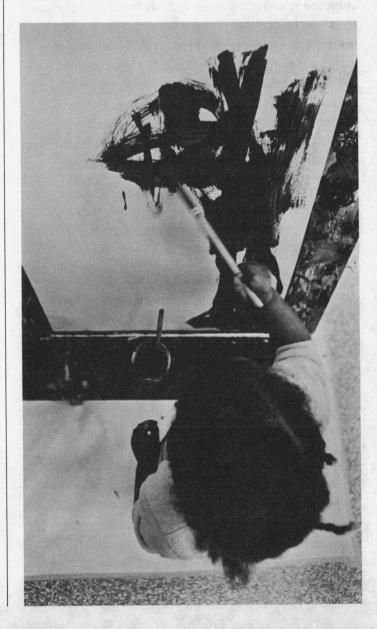

What can you learn at a LIBRARY?

A library includes more than the librarian who helps people find what they want. Behind the shelves of books and catalog cases is a whole group of people and things to learn from.

Administrators prepare the budget, plan for expanded service and new buildings, select, train, and oversee personnel. Specialists arrange exhibits, organize and conduct meetings, and coordinate library activities with other community activities. There are also artists and designers, public relations technicians, and community organizers. Someone decides which books, magazines, newspapers, pamphlets, films, and records to buy.

There are accountants and clerical help. There is someone to order materials and pay the bills, someone to follow up on lenders who have not returned books, someone to be in charge of security. There are also catalogers to designate the "classification number" and workers to print the cards and file them, cover new books with plastic jackets, insert pockets and cards in volumes, reshelve the books upon return, and repair or rebind damaged books. There are those who issue library cards and keep a careful record of new borrowers.

There are a maintenance crew and supervisors who can teach you about how to fix wires that need repair, a faulty ventilation system, or broken machinery, how to clean dirty halls, and how to trim untidy shrubs and bushes.

Ask the head librarian to tell you whom to talk to about the special machinery in the library, how it works, what it's for, and who maintains it. There may be a photographic book charging machine, which photographs a user's library card when he takes a book out; microfilm and microcard machinery; and pneumatic tubes or electric conveyors for transporting books from one part of the building to another.

There are also specialists in a library who can lead you not only to the proper written material but also to the proper person for more information. Some libraries stock books for the blind. Ask the person in charge about braille. How is it done? How is it taught? The talking book service is another interesting part of some libraries. Who records it? What are the copyright laws? What if a person doesn't have a record player or doesn't

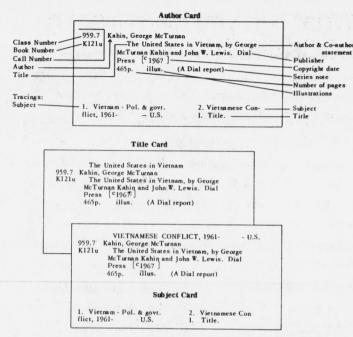

live in an area with a library that has these resources? Specialists in rare books are also a valuable source of information. How have printing techniques changed? Format? Content? How have book jackets changed? How is the worth of an old book determined?

Where can you find libraries? Call City Hall for the public library, see the phone book for branches or ask at the main desk for their branches. There are also libraries in schools and colleges, libraries for the armed forces, United States Information Libraries (over 160 libraries in over 65 countries around the world), newspaper libraries ("morgues") for every major newspaper, as well as special libraries established as part of a business firm or professional group, for example, a bank, pharmaceutical company, oil company, museum, or medical society. There are hospital libraries, where you can learn about special devices that put books on microfilm projected onto the ceiling and have a push-button device that changes the page, about prism glasses, which give right reading angles for a patient unable to move his head, and about mechanical page turners. A library may also be a consultant to a radio or television program and may sponsor reading classes for children.

Ask the main librarian or a person in adult services for the person who can help you in the building. Talk to architects about design needs for a library; talk to a lawyer about lawsuits against a library and laws governing the banning of books; talk to a publisher and librarians about changing tastes in books; talk to printers about typesetting and to graphic designers and psychologists about the effect of book cover design on selection.

What can you learn from a LOCKSMITH?

The job of a locksmith is the installation and opening of locks and the making of keys. You can find a locksmith by looking in the Yellow Pages or by contacting your local Locksmiths Association.

The locksmith is constantly studying new locking devices, both the electronic and key types. Manufacturers of locks often give seminars about their new equipment, and a convention is held once a year to bring locksmiths up to date. At these conventions various classes are held in such areas as key techniques by impression; locking devices in safes, given by the manufacturer of that safe; and setting up a master key system (in a large building, for example, there could be one key to open all offices, or one key per office, or a master key system). There is a safe school in Rochester, New York, where a locksmith learns to open a safe without knowing the combination. This course in manipulation is given by Sargent and Greenleaf, who are the original builders of safe locks.

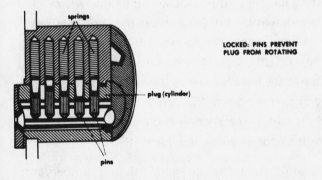

LOCKED: PINS PREVENT PLUG FROM ROTATING

plug (cylinder)

springs

pins

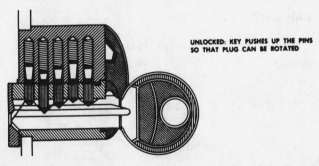

UNLOCKED: KEY PUSHES UP THE PINS SO THAT PLUG CAN BE ROTATED

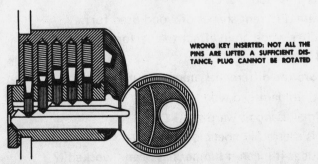

WRONG KEY INSERTED: NOT ALL THE PINS ARE LIFTED A SUFFICIENT DISTANCE; PLUG CANNOT BE ROTATED

I asked the locksmith I was interviewing what he was working on that interested him so much. He did not hesitate to tell me that his hobby was working on antique safes and that he was trying to open a safe from Anthony Wayne's house. He had been searching for a long, long time for a seven-inch key that could be fitted into a secret compartment of the side door of the safe. After having found a seven-inch key he made a new key from that one that would fit the lock. This process is called "making a key by impression." He went on to explain how this is done. First, put the key in the keyhole and twist it just hard enough to make a scratch on it. Remove it and file this scratch down until it is not seen any more when it is placed in the lock. These keys are usually made out of steel, but cast iron can be used.

I then asked him what he did when someone called to say that he had locked himself out of his house.

"Well, I come with my lock picks and a lock gun pick and try to open the door. The lock gun acts like a cue ball inside the lock, vibrating the pins in the lock, pushing them up and down. There's one kind of lock that has a mushroom pin in it that is very hard to open.

"After I get the lock open I remove it and make keys. If it is a foreign key and I don't have a blank for it, I make a rubbing of it and send it to Taylor's. They are the biggest place in the States for all keys from all over the world. Everyone goes to them. They are in Philadelphia. All the key blanks are numbered, and they have a complete record of all the keys."

I went on to ask him if he did much work with the police, and he told me he was often called in to investigate burglaries on safes and also robberies involving locks. His background included a course in Washington, D. C., given by Sargent and Greenleaf to the diplomatic corps under government orders. There he learned how to apply listening devices. Next came a refresher course in burglar alarms.

At that point he explained the tape method, by which all openings—doors, windows, and overhead openings—are sealed with a sort of magnetic tape. The alarm is set at night with a key in a special box. He added, "Many robbers buy the same stuff as the building owners and learn how to use it and then come in through the roof." He thought that was rather clever himself.

He also told me of his work with the Ford Motor Company. It seems that an increasingly profitable business is resulting from stealing from car trains—those long trains that haul nothing but new cars. They are often forced to park or wait in rather deserted areas and are prey for thieves. The keys are removed from the ignition, trunks are opened, and tires and other items are taken. Of course I asked why they didn't lock the cars and send all the keys ahead separately, but my locksmith only assured me that the cars would still be broken into and that it was far cheaper to replace a few items and hire a locksmith to make new keys than to have to have an entire car repaired.

I asked him more about electronic locks, and he informed me that they were primarily used only in high-security places and were known as cypher locks. To operate these you need a card or you need to push a lot of buttons.

There are several organizations that this locksmith belongs to: (1) Association of American Locksmiths, Inc., (2) National Locksmiths of America, (3) Safe Man's Association, and (4) Philadelphia Locksmiths Association, which has seminars once a month.

I asked him how he got started on all of this. "It started as a hobby. I worked for the Department of Justice; I was a cook at the Atlanta Prison, and in my time off I went and watched the staff work on the locks for the prison."

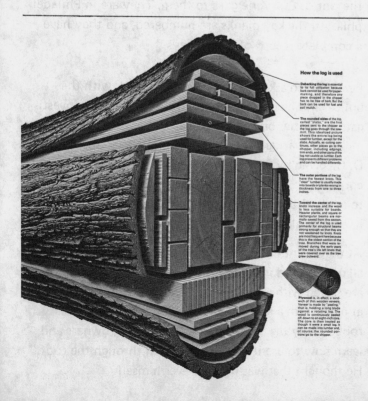

How the log is used

Debarking the log is essential to its full utilization because bark cannot be used for papermaking, and therefore any piece dropped in the chipper has to be free of bark. But the bark can be used for fuel and soil mulch.

The rounded sides of the log, called "slabs," are the first pieces sent to the chipper as the log goes through the sawmill. This idealized picture shows the entire log being used for lumber, except for the slabs. Actually, as cutting continues, other pieces go to the chipper, including edgings, trim ends, and other parts of the log not usable as lumber. Each log presents different problems and can be handled differently.

The outer portions of the log have the fewest knots. This "clear" lumber is usually made into boards or planks varying in thickness from one to three inches.

Toward the center of the log, knots increase and the wood is less suitable for boards. Heavier planks, and square or rectangular beams are normally sawed from this section. The center of the log is used primarily for structural beams strong enough so that they are not weakened by knots. Knots are most frequent here because this is the oldest section of the tree. Branches that were removed during the early years of the tree's life left knots that were covered over as the tree grew outward.

Plywood is, in effect, a sandwich of thin wooden veneers. Veneer is made by "peeling," that is, holding a long blade against a rotating log. The wood is continuously peeled off, down to an eight-inch core. The core is then treated as though it were a small log. It can be made into lumber and, of course, the rounded portions go to the chipper.

What can you learn at a LUMBERYARD?

Most of the houses in this country are built out of wood. For that reason alone, lumberyards are both prevalent and interesting. But even if you've never tried to build something in wood, you will learn a lot at a lumberyard about what wood is and where it comes from and how it's used.

Lumberyards are listed in the Yellow Pages of the telephone directory, so you can find one easily. Pick a time when they're not busy, so that the employees will have time to answer your questions. Not all of the people you find at a lumberyard will be teeming with information or anxious to talk. You may have to visit several lumberyards before you find someone who can assist you in your learning excursion. Keep trying. It will be worth the effort in the end.

A little understanding about lumber and its uses will open your eyes to things everywhere around you made out of wood that you probably overlook now. The most interesting lumberyard to visit would be one where they do mill work. Here you can see the various types of power equipment used to make doors, windows, paneling, and other specialized items. Of course, the best way to see how lumber is used is to watch a carpenter at work. The section "Carpenter" in this book tells you where to find a carpenter and gives some ideas about what to look for as you watch him.

Here are some questions you might ask at a lumberyard:

What is lumber?

What is the difference between kiln-dried wood and green wood?

What are the standard sizes of lumber?

Why is the actual size of a board different from its nominal size?

How are logs milled into boards?

How is plywood made?

What are different shapes of wood used for?

How does wood grain affect the performance of the board?

What are the differences among "warp," "wind," and "twist" in damaged wood?

What makes wood warp?

What is dressed lumber?

What does it mean if lumber has been "worked"?

What does the term "matched" mean with regard to lumber?

What is the difference between "hard wood" and "soft wood"?

What are the most popular kinds of wood?

What are the most popular sizes of wood?

Where do different kinds of wood grow?

Is lumber being used more or less today than in the past?

Are trees for lumber becoming scarce?

How has the price of lumber changed over the past several years?

How does a lumberyard operate?

What sizes of wood are delivered?

What resawing is done at the lumberyard?

How are different sizes and types of wood coded for easy finding?

How is lumber stored?

How is lumber moved around the lumberyard?

How is lumber delivered to customers?

Who buys lumber?

How is wood graded?

How is lumber priced?

Who determines the price?

What is meant by the term "board foot"?

How do you write an order for a board of a particular size, shape, and grade?

What milling is done at the lumberyard?

What tools are used at the lumberyard?

How does a radial arm saw operate?

What other things are sold at a lumberyard?

What are the different kinds of nails and screws?

What special purposes are served by each type of nail or screw?

How are nails sized and sold?

What is the difference between a "hollow core" and a "solid core" door?

What is a prehung door?

Why does plywood only come in certain sizes (mainly 4' x 8')?

What types of paneling are made?

What varieties of siding are available?

How are shutters made?

How are windows made?

What different types of molding are available?

What different kinds of roofing material exist?

What is sheetrock used for?

How does building insulation come from a factory?

What can you learn about MONEY?

How Is Money Made?

It is very interesting to watch coins being minted. There are two U.S. Mints that circulate coins, located in Philadelphia and Denver. There is also a mint in San Francisco, but coins are no longer made there for circulation, only for collectors and special issues. Tours are available at the mints.

Paper currency is printed by the Bureau of Printing and Engraving, which is a division of the U.S. Treasury in Washington, D. C.

Both coins and paper currency are distributed through the Federal Reserve Banks, which are located in cities throughout the country. You can identify the Federal Reserve Bank that issued the bills in your pocket by looking at the serial number. The prefix letter corresponds to the cities below. You will also see a black number in each of the corners of the bill; these, too, correspond to Federal Reserve Banks according to the following list.

Federal Reserve Bank	Letter	Number
Boston	A	1
New York	B	2
Philadelphia	C	3
Cleveland	D	4
Richmond	E	5
Atlanta	F	6
Chicago	G	7
Saint Louis	H	8
Minneapolis	I	9
Kansas City	J	10
Dallas	K	11
San Francisco	L	12

Visit a mint or a Federal Reserve Bank and find out how money is stored. How is money transported from the mint or the Treasury to banks?

How Is Money Counted?

To see automated counting machines and special ways of counting money, visit a bank, a race track with paramutual betting, the office of a vending machine company, or the place where parking meter money is taken.

What Was the Biggest Bank Robbery Ever?

According to the *Guinness Book of World Records,* the biggest bank robbery was 23,500,000 francs, which is equal to $4,770,000. The robbery was accomplished by force by 150 members of the Organisation de l'Armée Secrète (O.A.S.) from the Banque d'Algérie in Oran, Algeria.

The biggest "inside job" was performed in 1949 by an assistant manager of the National City Bank of New York, Richard Crowe. He removed $883,660 but was arrested shortly thereafter.

How Much Money Is There in the United States?
The following table shows the amount of money in circulation in the United States over the last thirty years.

U.S. MONEY IN CIRCULATION
SOURCE: U.S. Department of Treasury (in millions of dollars)

Denomination	1939	1945	1950	1959	1961	1965	1967	1968	1969
Coin	590	1,274	1,554	2,304	2,582	4,060	4,918	5,691	5,790
$1	559	1,039	1,113	1,511	1,588	1,818	2,035	2,049	1,989
$2	36	73	64	85	92	127	136	136	136
$5	1,019	2,313	2,049	2,216	2,313	2,489	2,850	2,993	2,882
$10	1,772	6,782	5,998	6,672	6,878	7,514	8,366	8,786	8,592
$20	1,576	9,201	8,529	10,476	10,935	12,974	15,162	16,508	16,531
$50	460	2,327	2,422	2,803	2,869	3,482	3,915	4,186	4,212
$100	919	4,220	5,043	5,913	6,106	8,092	9,311	10,068	10,259
$500	191	454	368	261	242	243	240	244	245
$1,000	425	801	588	341	300	286	285	292	292
$5,000	20	7	4	3	3	3	3	3	3
$10,000	32	24	12	5	10	4	4	4	4
Total	7,598	28,515	27,741	32,591	33,918	42,056	47,226	50,961	50,936

What Makes Money Valuable?
To find out how money becomes valuable and how its value changes, talk to an economist, a bank officer, a businessman, or an official of a savings and loan company.

How Much Money Is a Lot?
Consider the following facts about sums of money. Then decide for yourself how much money is a lot.

The average American wage-earner will earn a total of about $400,000 in his lifetime.

If you started with a penny tonight and put it into a jar and doubled it every night (putting in 2 cents tomorrow, 4 cents the next day, 8 cents the day after, and so on), you would have over a million dollars in less than a month. Figure it out! You would need a pretty large jar!

A million dollars ($1,000,000): If you and two of your friends started one year ago with a million dollars and each of you spent a thousand dollars every day ($1,000), you would have spent all of the money by today. Could you spend a thousand dollars every day for an entire year?

A billion dollars ($1,000,000,000): If the three captains of Columbus' ships started in 1492 with a billion dollars and each of them spent a thousand dollars a day, they

How to Make a Penny

A lot of people save pennies. Many more people just put them in a drawer and forget about them. That's too bad. Pennies are needed in the world of business. If all the forgotten pennies were brought out of hiding and used, it would save the mint a lot of time and money making more and more pennies every year.

In 1969 the mint made over five billion pennies. It was the first time in the mint's 178 year history that it had made so many pennies in one year. Pennies accounted for 76 percent of the total number of all the coins made last year. This year the mint plans to make 5½ billion pennies.

Pennies are made of two metals. They are 95 percent copper and 5 percent zinc. "Nickels" are also made of two metals. They are 75 percent copper but only 25 percent nickel.

All other coins are called composite coins because they are made in three layers. The outside layers are cupronickel and the middle layer is pure copper. Dimes, quarters and half-dollars all have three layers. The layers must be held together. This is called cladding.

The Philadelphia Mint has the best coinage equipment in the world including all the machines to make clad coins. The explanation of clad coins does not appear in this pamphlet but you will see the machines on your tour.

Commemorative and other special medals are also made at the Mint. These medals are made to honor an historic event, or a President, or a spectacular achievement.

MAKE-UP
The make-up box is weighed on a floor scale. It's called a make-up box because it holds the raw metal from which coins are made up. A big crane picks up the box and takes it to the melting furnace.

MELTING
The furnace is electric and gets red hot. When the metal is put inside the furnace it melts. The furnace is big enough to hold 15,000 pounds of metal.

CASTING
The melted metal is poured into a mold that looks like a giant candy bar. The bar is called an ingot. When the melted metal cools it gets hard again. The bar is about 18 feet long and weighs about 7,000 pounds.

CROPPING SAW
Each bar is cut in half. Now there are two bars. They are called slabs. Each one must be 8 and a half feet long and weigh 3,300 pounds. Any scrap is sent back to the furnace. Nothing is wasted.

REHEAT FURNACE
This is another electric furnace that heats the slab to just the right temperature so it will be soft enough to be rolled out.

ROLLING LINES
The slab is red hot and is six inches thick. Many things happen here:
First the slab squeezes through a pair of rollers. The rollers are so close together and press down so hard that when the slab comes out after several trips back and forth it is only one-half inch thick.

The rolled out slab is still red hot. It must be cooled to room temperature. Now it is sent through two sprays of water to cool it.
The top and bottom of the slab must be smooth. A machine shaves the top and bottom. The shavings go back to the melting furnace. The strip is now smooth and bright and so thin it can be rolled up into a coil.
Even though the coiled strip is very thin it is not thin enough. So the strip is uncoiled and put through a second rolling mill. When it comes out it is only a tenth of an inch thick.
When uncoiled the strip is about 400 feet long. Sometimes two or more of the uncoiled strips are welded together to make a strip even longer. Rough edges are trimmed off the strip to make it smooth. Now the coil is rolled down in the third rolling mill to one-twentieth of an inch thick, 15 inches wide.

INSPECTION, COUNTING AND BAGGING
At last we have a penny! Bad pennies are not allowed to leave the mint. Good pennies go to the counting machine. After 5,000 pennies fall into the bag a sewing machine sews the bag shut. The bags go to the Federal Reserve Bank. Then the pennies go to you.

COINING PRESS
The shiny golden penny blanks are ready to receive the impression of President Lincoln's portrait on one side and the Lincoln Memorial on the other. The designs are impressed from hard steel coinage dies onto the blank. Fingers on the press firmly grab each blank and one heavy blow stamps the design on each side.

UPSETTING MILLS
The blanks roll on their edges through this machine. They are soft enough so that when the machine presses on them it raises a rim around the blanks.

ANNEALING AND CLEANING LINES
The blanks are put into a gas furnace to be softened again. (Annealing means to soften). They come out of the furnace red hot and drop into water to cool. The blanks are then cleaned and polished. Then they are rinsed off with water and dried.

BLANKING PRESS
The strip is ready for punching out round pieces of metal about the size of a penny. They are called blanks, or planchets. This machine works just like a cookie cutter. After the blanks are punched out any strip left over is sent back to the make-up box.

would have spent only a little more than half of it by today ($525,600,000).

A trillion dollars ($1,000,000,000,000): If each of the three wise men started the year Christ was born with a trillion dollars (the approximate size of the annual United States Gross National Product) and they each spent a thousand dollars a day, by today they would have spent only 1/500 of the money ($2,159,340,000).

What Happens to Old, Worn-Out Money?
Damaged or mutilated coins are sent to the Assay Office of the U.S. Treasury in New York City, where they are destroyed.

On the average a dollar bill lasts only a year in circulation. A hundred-dollar bill may last as many as five years. When bills wear out, they are sent to a Federal Reserve Bank, where the numbers are checked and recorded so that new bills can be issued to replace them. Every day over $12 million in bills wear out. When the new bills are issued, a "star" prefix is placed on the serial number. A canceling machine perforates packages of worn-out bills to make sure they will not be used again. Then they are incinerated in special incinerators installed in the U.S. Treasury Department or the Federal Reserve Bank branches.

How Does Money Earn Money?
To find the answer to this question, talk to an economist, a bank officer, a savings and loan company officer, a stock broker, an investment counselor, a real estate broker, an accountant, a successful businessman, or an officer of a mutual fund.

More about Money
Find an introductory book on money in the library and look up the history of money. How old is money? What did people use before there was money? What are the alternatives to money today? How does a credit card work as money? Do you think there will ever be a time when people won't use money anymore?

Gold standard. The standard of value which many nations have adopted when regulating the value of their monetary units. It has been said that the only true money is gold and all else is but a token of money. But in recent times it has been realised the value of money depends more upon the supply available and the demand of those willing to hold it. As long as supply is sufficiently limited and the people have sufficient confidence in the stability of its value *per unit* (in terms of goods and services), this value will tend to be maintained.

What can you learn at a MUSEUM?

The Impressionist painting: "They're staring at me . . . more and more of them. How divine. Perhaps it is true that interest in museums is heightening. People who have never wandered through here and appreciated my beauty are certainly missing out on something. Admittedly, I am a very fine example of Impressionism—a style of painting that gave birth to modern art in the late 1800s.

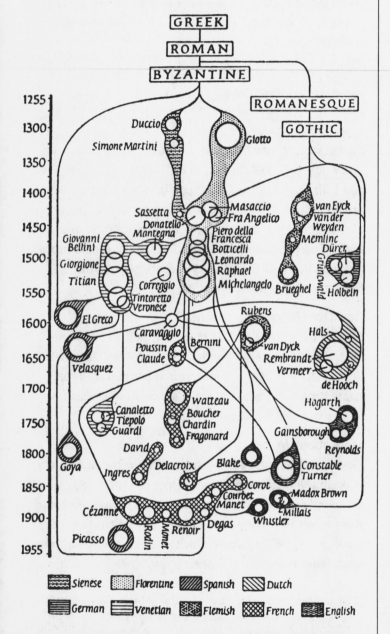

GREEK
ROMAN
BYZANTINE
ROMANESQUE
GOTHIC

1255
1300 — Duccio, Giotto
Simone Martini
1350
1400 — Sassetta, Masaccio Fra Angelico, van Eyck van der Weyden
1450 — Donatello Mantegna, Piero della Francesca, Memlinc Dürer
Giovanni Bellini, Botticelli
1500 — Giorgione, Leonardo Raphael, Grünewald
Titian, Correggio, Michelangelo, Brueghel Holbein
1550 — Tintoretto Veronese
El Greco, Rubens
1600 — Caravaggio, Hals
Poussin Claude, Bernini, van Dyck Rembrandt Vermeer
1650 — Velasquez, de Hooch
1700 — Watteau, Hogarth
Canaletto Tiepolo Guardi, Boucher Chardin Fragonard, Gainsborough
1750
David, Reynolds
1800 — Goya, Delacroix, Blake, Constable Turner
Ingres
1850 — Corot, Madox Brown
Courbet Manet, Millais
Cézanne, Degas, Whistler
1900 — Picasso, Rodin, Renoir
Monet
1955

Sienese Florentine Spanish Dutch
German Venetian Flemish French English

"While people look at me, are they aware of the names of the artists involved in the Impressionist movement? Monet, for example, was credited with the art of seeing something as it really was, instead of looking through a screen of past art forms. Most people see by way of their parents or the social milieu in which they live.

Sometimes, though, on a youthful morning, the curtains fall from their eyes and the world appears. I bet many young people would understand what I mean.

"Other artists, contemporaries of Monet—geniuses like Renoir, Manet, Degas, Cézanne, Toulouse-Lautrec, and Van Gogh—were also nonconformists who created this new method of seeing and expressing the world around them, breaking sharply with the art preceding them. When people look at their works, do they see that they are characterized chiefly by short brush strokes of bright colors that achieve the effect of light on objects? From a distance these works look different than they do close up. The brush strokes produce subtle impressions of the object being painted. They leave it to the eye to stand back and create the whole picture.

"But it's not enough merely to appreciate the painting. The viewer should seek to find out more about the revolutionary techniques introduced by these artists and about their experimentation and success with light and color. Also important to investigate is their optimistic rendering of the simple pleasures of life, such as eating in a tavern or at a picnic or bathing in the ocean. These are ideas that everyone can understand.

"Museum guides can answer questions about the resistance in art circles to Impressionist painting. The origins of the painters and their works and the changes they underwent are fascinating. Many museums and local colleges offer lectures on Impressionism. And many museums give painting courses where an art lover can try his hand at emulating the old masters or starting a revolution of his own in the art world."

The Greek statue: "Few works can surpass me in age and influence, for I date back to ancient Greece between the fourth and fifth centuries B.C. and am one of the first examples of balanced composition, the natural rendering of anatomical details and the distribution of weight in a figure. Specifically, with my creation man finally made a statue look like man—a beautiful, classic man. Nowadays when people speak about the classical age, they refer to me and other statues like me.

"For people more interested in history or archaeology than in art, I am still a jumping-off point, for I echo the history of a country and an age. When the Romans conquered Greece, I became part of their booty. On the trip to Rome, however, the ship and I sank in a storm. Eventually, about twenty-two centuries later, local

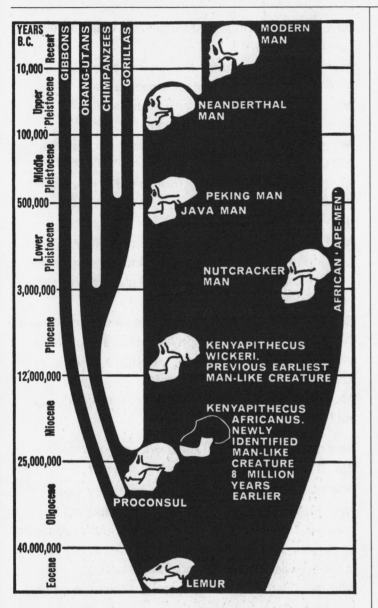

fishermen who had discovered me hidden on the shores under centuries of sand pointed me out to archaeologists.

"A tour guide or library book could answer questions about the influence I have had even up to present times, the climate of Greece that enabled me to be created, and about the other artists of the day, such as architects and poets, who were also creating classical standards in their respective fields."

Most large cities have museums, easily located in the telephone book. And most cities have their own history and local artists. As a result, even a small town's past may be collected in a museum that is filled with works by local artists, as well as two centuries of American arts and artifacts. New England towns boast whaling museums with works carved in whalebone. Towns dating back to colonial days have museums full of Americana. And often they are manned by someone who knows details long forgotten by other folk.

What can you learn at a NEWSPAPER PLANT?

Newspapers appear at the newsstand or at our doorstep with such regularity that we tend to take them for granted. Like telephones, mail delivery, and many other products and services we use every day, we have come to depend heavily on newspapers without really understanding how they are put together or how they affect our lives.

If you want to treat yourself to an exciting learning experience, visit the newspaper plant in your city. Most newspapers conduct guided tours of their facilities, but if they do not provide this service on a regular basis, they will probably be glad to show you around on request. After touring the newspaper plant, you will stop taking the newspaper for granted, and you will have learned many new things. Moreover, you will come to understand why veteran newspapermen refer to the newspaper production process (with genuine affection and only slight understatement) as the "daily miracle."

You will see how team effort combines the many talents of telephone operators, secretarial and clerical staffs, artists, accounting personnel, maintenance people, writers, photographers, editors, and reporters. You will have an opportunity to examine the role newspapers play in a democratic society and to understand the importance of freedom of the press. You will gain insight into what Thomas Jefferson meant when he said, "Were it left to me to decide whether we should have government without newspapers, or newspapers without government, I should not hesitate to prefer the latter."

In the news room you will see how scores of reporters, editors, rewrite men and women, and feature writers collaborate to track down, verify, research, write, and edit news stories. (For more details about the kind of work these men and women do , see "Journalist" in this book.) You can visit the library, or "morgue," and find out how millions of "dead" news clippings and huge amounts of reference material are stored for future use. You can see how headlines are prepared and watch the teletype machines send out news and receive stories over the wire service lines that link news centers throughout the world. Listen carefully to the terminology used around the newspaper plant, for you will be introduced to a fascinating new language of newspaper people.

Visit the composing room and see how news stories are set in type by linotype operators using large typesetting machines. You will learn how these machines set lines of type and recycle the lead to be reused time and time again. You will see how photographs undergo special processing so that they can be reproduced as images composed of thousands of tiny dots. You will find out how drawings and illustrations are converted to printing plates for reproduction. How are the stories and photographs put together to form whole pages where everything fits without wasting space? (For added information about newspaper pictures, see "Photography" in this book.)

IMPRESSION ROLLER
PLATE CYLINDER
INK ROLLER

ROLL OF PAPER

Diagram of a 6-unit newspaper printing press

One of the most interesting things to see at a newspaper plant is the press room. Here you will see giant rotary presses capable of operating at speeds up to 45 miles per hour to produce thousands of newspapers an hour. From enormous rolls of paper, newspapers are printed, cut, folded, and assembled in a single operation that takes less than a minute. The scale, layout, and performance of the press room are truly impressive.

Here are some questions you might ask your tour guide or the people you see working at the newspaper plant:

How are newspapers produced?
How much paper is required daily to produce the newspaper?
How is the paper delivered, stored, and moved around the plant?
Where does the paper come from?
How are the printing plates made?
How are the presses kept in good working order?
What happens when one of the presses breaks down?
How are the color sections of the newspaper printed?
How much ink is required daily to print the paper?

How are the individual tasks organized in the production operation?
Who is chiefly responsible for major decisions?
How does the circulation department operate?
What does the promotion department do?
What does the personnel department do?
Where and how do the employees learn the required skills?
What is the range of jobs performed at the newspaper?
How is the staff hired?
How is the news room organized?
What are the physical working conditions like?
How are the newspapers distributed to the customers?
How are the photographs taken and prepared for publication?
How is the newspaper continually designed and changed?
Can you trace the production process of a single news story from its birth as a news tip until it appears as a story in the paper at the newsstand?
What other vital roles must be performed to get a paper out?

How do the economics of the newspaper operate?
How is the price determined for the newspaper?
How many employees are required to run the paper?
What is the aggregate payroll for the newspaper?
What role does advertising revenue play in the economics of the newspaper?
Is the newspaper making a profit or a loss?
Who monitors the financial success of the paper? How?

What role does the editorial policy play in the newspaper?
Who determines the editorial policy?
In what form is the editorial policy presented?
How does the editorial policy affect the handling of news stories?
What are the goals of the newspaper?
Does the editorial policy affect circulation?

Other interesting questions:
What public service functions are performed by the newspaper?
How has the role of the newspaper in society changed over time?
In what ways does the newspaper get recognized for excellence?
Who owns the newspaper?
How does the newspaper view the role of freedom of the press?

What can you learn from your NEXT-DOOR NEIGHBOR?

The genius of the United States is not the best or most in its executives or legislators, nor in its ambassadors or authors or colleges or churches or parlors, nor even in its newspapers or inventors . . . but always most in the common people.
—Walt Whitman

We've included your next-door neighbor as a learning resource to remind you again not to overlook the most obvious opportunities. You can learn something from everybody. Ask questions, and become a good listener. There's a delicate balance between learning and being nosy—some people may be sensitive to certain questions. Use your judgment, but use your curiosity as well. As Dorothy Parker once wrote, "People are more fun than anybody."

Here are some questions to start with:

Where did you grow up?
Where did you go to school?
What did you study?
What are your favorite memories of growing up?
How did you learn the things you know?

What do you do for a living?
Where did you learn to do it?
How did you decide to do this kind of work?
What skills does it take to do your job well?
What kinds of people do you work with?

What interests do you have?
What hobbies do you have?
How do you spend your vacations?
Have you ever traveled anywhere interesting?
What was it like there?
If you were ever in the service, what did you do, and what was it like?
What do you do for entertainment?

What are your plans for the future?
If you could have any wish, what would you wish for?
What would you most like to see changed about the world?

Although we usually think of neighbors as people, places and processes near you also act as neighbors and are valuable learning resources, too.

What can you learn from an ORCHESTRA MEMBER?

An orchestra cannot be found in every town or city, but you can watch for a visiting group or talk to musicians in local symphonies, to music teachers or free-lance musicians, to music directors at radio or television stations, or to music librarians at the stations or in the library. Check for music teachers in your local public or private schools, settlement houses, and local colleges or write to the following organization for information:
American Federation of Musicians (AFL-CIO)
641 Lexington Avenue
New York, New York 10022

An orchestra member can be a musician, conductor, business manager, publicity director, lawyer, member of the board of directors, treasurer or accountant, head of volunteers, special affairs assistant, or one of those people affiliated with the symphony hall, like ushers, ticket collectors, acoustical engineers, stage crew, clerical staff, promotion personnel, fund raisers, travel managers, instrument tuners, and maintenance staff. There are also people who are peripherally affiliated, like public relations personnel, printers, music critics, record companies, television and radio crews, and, of course, the audience.

From a musician you can learn about music and instruments. Most musicians play more than one instrument and should be familiar with the history, the care, and the different uses and sounds of those instruments. The musician should also be able to introduce you to composers—their lives and the music they wrote for those instruments.

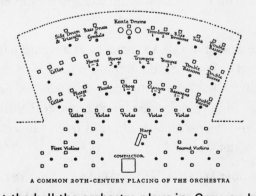

A COMMON 20TH-CENTURY PLACING OF THE ORCHESTRA

Look at the hall the orchestra plays in. Can you hear and see from all angles of the room? Was the hall built especially for concerts or is it used for something else, like a church or a gym? Check with an acoustical engineer and an architect about how to build buildings to ensure a good seat for all the concert-goers. How do the building materials and the shape and size of the building influence the acoustics? Has the building changed over the years? How? What are the great concert halls of the world?

Who organizes a concert tour? Who makes certain that the right number of chairs is set up and the proper chair formation executed? Who selects the music to be played? What is the role of a conductor? What is the role of the assistant conductor? What is the difference between the first violinist and the other violinists?

Who manages an orchestra? Who hires and fires, and who raises the money to pay the orchestra members?

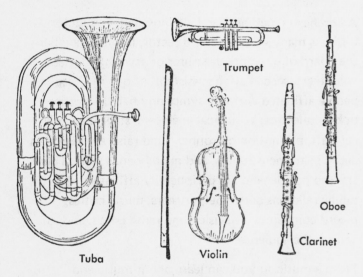

Trumpet

Tuba

Violin

Clarinet

Oboe

How much of the operating budget comes from the sales of tickets and how much from other sources?

What is the job market for a musician who wants to play with an orchestra professionally? How many of these aspirants hold down other jobs and play in civic orchestras for either little or no pay and mostly enjoyment?

If possible, visit or talk to someone at a record company. What kind of contracts do orchestras have with the record companies? How is the individual member paid? Are there union regulations for an orchestra? How are salaries and the percentage of profit from a successful recording determined?

Any member (direct or indirect) of an orchestra can lead you to other sources of information. Although most professional musical activities take place in large cities, almost every town has at least one private music teacher or perhaps an accomplished church organist who can help you.

What can you learn at a PAPER BOX FACTORY?

I had always wanted to visit a factory, so when the opportunity came to visit a paper box factory, I jumped at the chance.

The factory I visited makes folding boxes—boxes that are stored flat and can be popped up to hold things like candy bars, baked goods, or paper towels. The first thing I noticed when I walked onto the production floor was the clamor of giant machines and the unusual odors that permeated the air. As far as my eye could see there was intense activity—people and machines busily working together with almost unbelievable efficiency. The harmony of manufacturing is indeed something to behold.

The production area of this factory covers an entire city block, with the management offices on the second floor above the plant area. The floor itself is divided into areas where specialized parts of the manufacturing process are performed. In one area giant cardboard rolls are unloaded from tractor-trailers and stored until they are needed. Most of the material that has to be moved around the plant is placed on "skids," which are wooden pallets elevated about six inches from the ground. A man using a motorized hand truck with two large fork-like extensions can lift a skid weighing several hundred pounds and move it easily anywhere in the factory.

In another area enormous printing machines take rolls of the cardboard and print package designs and product information onto them as they are unrolled from one spindle to another. Next, special machines punch the flattened boxes out of the rolled cardboard sheeting and score or perforate those places where folds will eventually be made. If cellophane is required, these machines can also punch windows into the cardboard and glue cellophane over the hole in a single operation. Operators stand by the machines and load the rolls into them, but all of the work is done automatically.

Occasionally, a roll will break or a machine will jam. In seconds, an incredible pile of waste cardboard is spewed out of the machine before the operator can shut it off. Nothing is wasted in a factory if it can be saved. Sweepers collect the scrap cardboard and take it to a large baling machine, where under great pressure big bales of waste paper are made. These are sold to scrap dealers to be used eventually in making new cardboard.

After the flattened box set-ups are finished, they are put into folding and gluing machines, where in a matter of seconds finished boxes start coming out the other end. These machines work so fast that they challenge your eye to make sense of what's happening.

Inspectors check and count the boxes before passing them down a conveyor belt to packers, who put them in cartons and label them for later identification. The full cartons are placed on skids that hold twenty cartons. Then they are moved into a warehouse to await trucks that will deliver them to the customers.

In many ways, most factories are similar. The really interesting parts of a manufacturing process are the ways materials are moved around the factory, how the specialized machines work, how quality control and inspections are carried out, and the overall layout of the plant. Most modern plants are highly automated and require specialized people to control and monitor the production process. Everywhere you see machines doing things that you would have thought only people could do—and doing it faster and better. It's really interesting to speculate on why machines haven't been invented to do those few jobs in a factory that people still do. Read the section "Union Boss" in this book, and ask about the existence and power of unions in this factory.

Wherever you live, there are factories of some sort nearby. Whether they make phonograph records, radios, shredded wheat, light bulbs, matches, or paper boxes, you will find them fascinating. Your local chamber of commerce or city tourist bureau should have lists of plants that regularly give tours. Frequently they will also give free samples of whatever they manufacture. But, even if you cannot find a factory near you that offers tours, you can often get to see the manufacturing process by contacting the public relations office of the company.

After visiting the plant, you may be inspired to delve into some books on the subject to learn about the historical evolution of the product or process you have just observed. It's especially interesting to learn how critical inventions, and usually very recent ones, have made what you have just viewed possible.

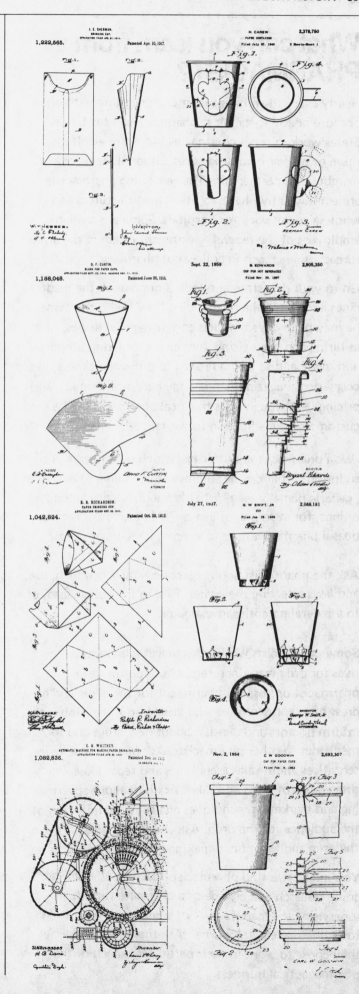

What can you learn from a PHARMACIST?

Nearly every town has at least one drugstore with one or more pharmacists. Most pharmacists in the United States work in retail pharmacies. About one-half of these own their own drugstores, either alone or as a member of a partnership. The remaining pharmacists are employed by pharmaceutical manufacturers and wholesalers or work for hospitals. Some are civilian employees of the federal government or are in the armed forces; others teach in colleges of pharmacy.

Go to your drugstore and look around at all the medicines and watch the pharmacist. If he is also the owner, he may be involved in sales and managerial duties, such as hiring and supervising sales clerks, ordering supplies and merchandise (some related to drugs and others, like cosmetics, magazines, and candy bars, not related), and pricing. How much does the local pharmacist advise his customers on medication for certain ailments?

Ask a pharmacist about drugs. Which ones need a prescription? What can be sold over the counter? What does "generic name" mean? What is the difference among brands, for example, of aspirin? What kinds of records does a pharmacist have to keep of his sales of drugs?

Ask the pharmacist about narcotics—their handling, use, and laws affecting their sale. Talk to the police, also, or to a federal narcotics investigator.

Some pharmacists work as technical sales representatives for drug manufacturers. (Ask your drugstore pharmacist or hospital pharmacist for the name and address of a representative who visits him.) Their job is to inform doctors and dentists about new drugs and to sell medicines to other pharmacists. Ask one of these representatives about sales techniques and record-keeping procedures of visits and sales. Ask him about advertising and marketing techniques and the determination of the audience for the drug. Ask about the "mark up" on the drug and the money-making aspect of the business.

You might also find pharmacists teaching at a college, doing research at a college or a pharmaceutical firm, supervising the manufacture of a new drug, or writing for a pharmaceutical journal. Ask them how and why they chose to work in their particular branch of the pharmaceutical business.

What can you learn about PHOTOGRAPHY?

Photography is a kind of chemical magic. If you have a friend who does photography as a hobby, ask if you can join him in the darkroom to see how the "magic" works. After you understand the principles, you'll find that basic photography is really simple.

In addition to its value as a hobby and its use in recording vacations and family get-togethers, photography has a wide range of important uses in the city. Visit a photographer's studio and learn how portraits are made. Ask the photographer how he retouches photographs and what special techniques he uses in producing unusual photographs. Learn about lighting and how different cameras and different lenses are used.

Go to a newspaper plant, and find out how photographs are converted into images that can be printed in your daily newspaper. (For ways to find a newspaper plant and things to look for, see "Newspaper Plant" in this book.) Ask how color photographs are printed. Do newspaper photographers use special kinds of cameras?

Visit a photographic laboratory where they develop and print many different kinds of film and photographs. Here you can learn about the intricacies of developing and printing. How are slides developed? How are large color prints made? What kinds of special equipment are needed for large-scale photographic work? What are the different chemicals used for developing, and where do they come from? How do specialists learn the skills required to work in a photography lab? What systems are employed to keep track of the photographs? What makes a professional print "good"?

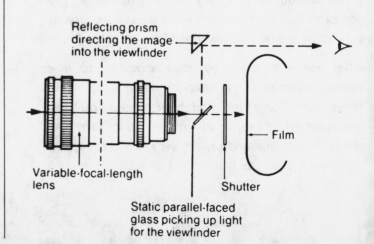

Reflecting prism directing the image into the viewfinder

Variable-focal-length lens

Static parallel-faced glass picking up light for the viewfinder

Shutter

Film

Go to an advertising agency and ask if they will allow you to watch a photographer prepare photographs for an advertising spread. Ask about special techniques for making products look especially attractive in color photographs. How do they photograph food? How are products shown off in particularly flattering light? How are fashion photographs made?

Visit the police laboratory in your city, where you will learn that photography is an important tool in crime detection and prevention. How are mug shots used for police records? What other special techniques do police photographers use?

Another important use of photography is television. Visit a television studio, and learn how television cameras work. How are newsreels prepared? What special uses of photography can you find at the television studio?

Here are some other things you can do to learn more about photography:
1. Visit a camera store to examine the range of available photographic equipment.
2. Visit a movie-making studio or watch a film crew on location to see how motion pictures are made.
3. Attend a photography exhibit to see how photography is used as a fine art medium.
4. Visit an industrial plant where photography is used as a tool in monitoring production processes or in quality control.
5. Take pictures yourself and learn to develop them.

After having done some of these things, you may come to understand what is meant by the saying "One picture is worth a thousand words." And, you will undoubtedly understand what makes the "magic" in the photographic process. You may even be on your way to taking up photography as a hobby.

What can you learn from a POST OFFICE AND POSTMAN?

I went into the post office in my small town of 16,000 people and went right up to the stamp lady at the big window. She knew me by sight and nodded as I approached. I explained about the *Yellow Pages* book, and she said without the slightest hesitation, "Sounds great, but the person you want to see about all these questions is the general manager." In a minute the door on the side of the room was opened, and I was shown into a room that looked like an old freight office: green walls and government-issue sturdy wood desks.

The general manager sat up while I explained the book and my sudden interest in the post office and its operations. Then he reclined in his office chair, one of those that almost seems to throw you over but for a quick foot catching on the bottom of the desk.

"How many people do you have working at the post office here?" I asked.

"Fifty-eight employees. They're all civil servants and have taken the Civil Service exams. But those exams won't be given any more now with the new U.S. Postal Service. The service will have its own exam and postal service ratings."

"Tell me how a typical day might go at the post office."

"Well, we open at 4:00 A.M. A tractor trailer pulls in from Norristown or from the sectional office in Philadelphia. The tractor trailer comes here, and the mail clerks unload the truck. The mail is in pouches— those large white bags. The clerks have the keys to the locks on the pouches. The clerks sort the mail inside by carriers. This sorting is done by hand. Then the carriers come in, and each carrier sorts his mail into sections.

"There are four ways of delivering mail:
1. Relay: The carrier takes about 35 pounds of mail at a time. A mail truck goes around and leaves pouches of mail at different boxes that the carrier has on his route. When he finishes one 35-pound pouch he stops and picks up another.

2. Park and loop routes: Here the mailman has all the mail with him in his truck. He parks the truck and gets

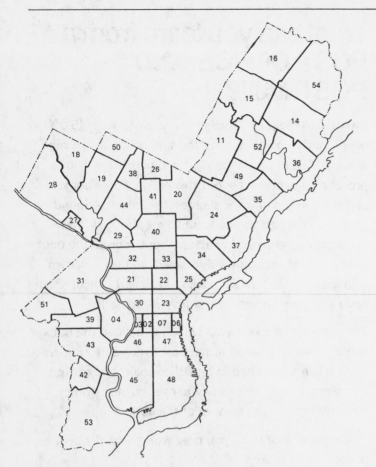

out and delivers a bit of mail, then hops in again and proceeds to the next stop, where he does another loop and then moves on.

3. Mounted carrier: This mail person goes out in a vehicle that is paid for by the government and puts the mail into individual mailboxes along the road.

4. Rural carrier: This carrier must provide his own vehicle to cover his route. He is reimbursed so much money per day per mile by the U.S. Postal Service."

The general manager also told me that most people employed by the Postal Service work eight hours a day, but there are many part-time employees and seasonal workers. When I asked about the different kinds of stamps, he told me that there is no set pattern for how and when new stamps are released. Yesterday I saw a postman and asked him about his job. "Lady," he said, "I got two minutes at a stop."

"So when do I interview you?"

"At lunch!"

But where does a postman eat lunch? I wondered.

So today I stopped another city postman who was ambling along. He was on his lunch break and had time to chat.

"I work a 40-hour week. I get up at 4:00 A.M. and get down to 9th and Market at 5:15. The clerks have already sorted the mail into routes. I pick up mine and sort it and bundle it in separate bundles for each street number. By 8:00 I'm ready to go. I have a partner on my route, which is one block and a half. I make two trips a day. Oh, I could tell you so much. Why don't you come down to 9th and Market some morning and watch?"

"I think I will," I said.

What can you learn from a PSYCHOLOGIST?

There are many different kinds of psychologists, and they can be found in many different places. A large percentage are found on college campuses, as instructors and as employees in the counseling department. Others work for government agencies, schools, hospitals, private industry (call the personnel office), nonprofit organizations, and clinics. Still others, in private practice, are listed in your local phone book.

Ask the psychologist what he does. Do you teach? Do you counsel individuals or work with groups? How is your work different from that of a social worker? Do you plan and conduct training programs for workers in industry? Do you do research? Do you administer psychology programs in a clinic, hospital, or research lab? Do you do psychological testing? What kind? What are these tests designed to show? Who takes them? How are they assessed?

Ask the psychologist how he obtains information about the person's traits, capabilities, and behavior. Do you interview? What kind of questions do you ask? Do you give a client your opinion about his answer? Do you study personal histories? How do you obtain a personal history? What does it tell you? Do you conduct controlled experiments? Where? For what? How do you record the results? Do you conduct surveys? What are the different kinds of surveys? What are they used for? How do you collect the information? How do you phrase the questions? What is a closed question and what is an open-ended one? How do you analyze the results?

What kind of routine administrative duties does a psychologist have to do? If he is in private practice, does he advertise? If so, how? How does he get his clients?

What can you learn about a QUARRY?

If you want to visit a quarry and you live in the center of a city, you're going to have to make a bit of an effort to see one in action, but it is well worth it if you like to be outside and see the inside of the earth. Here is how I got to one: There was a large construction job going on in the middle of the city. One day as I was going by there were ten concrete mixers lined up ready to pour. I started talking to one of the drivers and he told me that they came from a quarry about thirty miles from the city but that the company had a center-city business office. As it turned out, I knew someone who worked in this office who knew the workings of the quarry inside out. I phoned him and arranged to meet for lunch. I asked him, "If I hadn't known you, how would I have gotten to see a quarry?"

"You could always call the general manager or the plant manager and make arrangements to go and see the quarry," he told me.

He had a wealth of information about the processing of lime and limestone, which was the kind of quarry he worked with. I knew nothing, so he began at the beginning.

"First the workers go down into the quarry and drill rows of holes. These holes are about six inches in diameter and about six to eight feet apart. These holes are loaded with dynamite. When the blast is set off it brings down the stone in large hunks. Down there we have a ball much like the kind you see used for wrecking houses. We bust up the big boulders into a size that a front-end loader can load into trucks. The trucks haul them over to what is called the primary crusher. We call this the jaw crusher. From there they go up on a conveyor belt to the secondary crusher up on ground level. Here the stone is crushed again and screened to whatever application is called for. One and one-half inches is the size used for calcining (that is, the making of quick lime). All kinds of fascinating things happen to the stone depending on exactly what product you want to sell.

"Different types of quarries produce different kinds of stone. And different stones contain different amounts of minerals that make them more or less suitable for spe-cific uses. In limestone quarries there are two essentially different types. One is high-calcium limestone (calcium carbonate). This kind comes from the famous Bellefonte Ledge, which contains the largest and purest deposit of high-calcium limestone in the Eastern United States. The other kind is dolomitic limestone (calcium-magnesium carbonate).

"There are also other kinds of quarries to go and see. Granite, sandstone, traprock, and serpentine quarries are only a few of the kinds you might see."

(For other learning opportunities in the construction business, see "Bricklayer" and "Construction Site" in this book.)

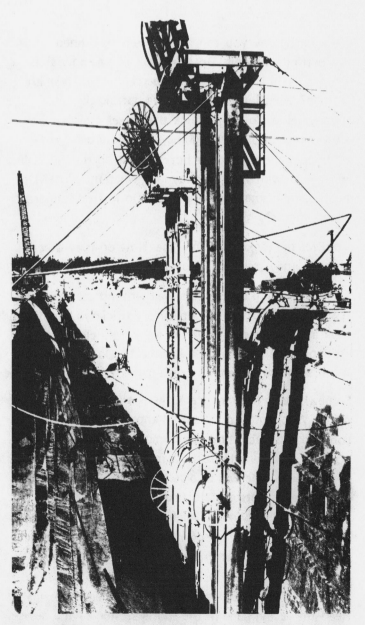

WIRE SAWS OPERATING IN A GRANITE QUARRY IN MASSACHUSETTS

What can you learn at a RACE TRACK?

A race track is a wild, hysterical, exciting place. Nowhere else can you see such extremes of emotion at the same time. No one walks at a race track. *Everyone* races—to the entrance gate, to the betting windows, to the hot dog stands, to his seat. People race toward a dream of sudden riches—of winning a long shot and leaving the track with more money than they've ever had before. The worst time to learn about a race track is on a racing day. Everyone is too frantic to talk. But any other day, when the horses are being exercised and the hot dogs are being delivered, there are lots of people who can explain the betting systems, the theory of probability, and the special lingo that is used, for example, words like *place* and *show.*

On a racing day you can watch the people lined up at the betting windows. Do they look like gamblers? Is there a "gambling type"? What percentage of them are women? What kind of people are betting the most money? How do people pick the horses they bet on? How many couples are arguing about their bets? How do people cheer for their horse? What do they look like when they win? How do they look when they lose? Do people come singly or in groups? Do losers bet more than winners?

Look at the jockeys in the race. How do they dress? How do they treat their horses?

On a non-racing day, take a walk around the track. Is it soft or hard? Is it dirt or some artificial material? Go look at the stables. Are they clean? Who cleans them? Ask someone how much a horse eats. Does he race on a full stomach? How is a horse named?

Somewhere at the race track there will be a manager's office. Whoever is in there will know how many people come to the track, how much money is lost and won, how the track was built, how much it cost, and how it is maintained. He will also tell you how much of the money he collects goes to taxes, how jockeys are trained, what they must weigh, and what they must eat on their special diets. You might also ask the manager about the techniques that are used to advertise the track. When so many of the people who go lose their money there, how does the track lure them back again? Read the racing page in the sports section of the newspaper a few times. See which horses win most frequently and which lose more often than they win. Are there any horses that do especially well on rainy days, when the track is wet and slippery?

What are the laws in your state about betting? Why are some people (usually minors) not allowed to bet? If you could bet, would you depend on instinct, or would you try to figure out a scientific or mathematical method? What do you think about the practice of betting? Is it worth the risk?

Brandywine Results

1ST—$1,600, C-3 pace, 1 mi.
Mr. Trapp (Wilcutts)   28.40   7.80   4.60
Leda Lobell (A. Myer)   3.00   2.60
Wheelsie (Lighthill)   3.00
   Off 8:02 Time 2:04.
   Also started—Bye Bye Eleanor, Phyllis Marie M., Daring Byrd, Keystone Mystic, Yankee Chief.

2D—$1,600, 3-yr-old mdns., pace. 1 mi.
Frank Blades (Anderson) 56.40 12.20 4.80
Farm Bell (V. Dancer)   2.60   2.60
Dance Band (G. Cameron)   3.60
   Off 8:21. Time 2:06 1-5.
   Also started—Rich Direct, Miss Anchor W., Jolie Madam, Afton Bonus, Lady Von Teck.
    Daily Double (2-5) Paid $378.20

3RD—$2,000, C-2 pace, 1 mi.
Mommy Song (A. Myer) 11.60 5.80 3.00
Rodel Beth (Parker)   5.60   3.80
Brad Weiover (Hylan)   2.40
   Off 8:43. Time 2:03 3-5.
   Also started—Eve's Mr. Keene, Butram, Lloyd Lawrence, Marland Jennie, Triple H. Pride.

4TH—$2,000, C-2 pace, 1 mi.
Freedom Chick (Myers) 12.60 4.60 3.40
Mr. Young (Wilcutts)   5.20   3.40
Fashion Row (Larente)   2.80
   Off 9:09. Time 2:01 4-5.
   Also started—Pipersville Val, Tee's Knight, Raven Lady, Gambrie.
    Scratched—Hello Yankee.
     Exacta (1-7) Paid $102.20

5TH—$4,100, clmg., pace 1 mi.
Rebel Liner (Greene)   4.80   3.20   2.40
Diamond M. Harry (Imel)   3.20   2.60
Robert Bruce N. (Bergeron)   3.60
   Off 9:31. Time 2:01 4-5.
   Also started—Wooster's Miracle, Bomber's Bomber, Kimberly Royal, Mister Duff, Coastman.

6TH—$2,500, C-1 pace, 1 mi.
Parson's Bret (Wilcutts)   4.00   2.60   2.40
G. B. Express (E. Davis)   4.00   3.20
Fighter Wave (S. King, Jr.)   4.20
   Off 9:50. Time 2:02 2-5.

What can you learn from a REAL ESTATE BROKER?

There are several ways to locate a real estate broker. You can (1) look in the Yellow Pages under "Realtor," (2) call your local real estate board, (3) call City Hall and ask for the Licenses and Inspection Department, (4) look at FOR SALE or FOR RENT signs outside of buildings or houses, (5) look in your newspaper's want ads under "Real Estate," (6) check with a Notary Public, (7) call your landlord, or (8) check with a homeowner's association. Here are some questions you might ask the broker you find:

How did you become a broker? Are you licensed? What does a license allow you to do? Do you have to have a certain educational background? Are there state or federal laws governing licensing?

How do you determine your clientele? Do you search out what they want or do they come to look at what you have? Do you advertise? How? What kind of property do you handle—land, apartments, homes, commercial buildings?

How are you paid? Do you receive a standard percentage of what you sell? Who else shares in the cost of the property? Do you also manage or rent buildings? Do you determine rent or cost of property? Do you also handle mortgages, loans, or insurance? Do you make property appraisals or help development of building projects?

How has the market changed? Is there a building boom? Is there enough office space in your town? Why have land prices increased? What effects do politics and economic conditions have on you? How is your work affected by zoning regulations? (See the section entitled "Zoning" in this book.)

Whom do you work with? Are you a one-man office? Do you work for someone else? Do you hire other people to help you—secretaries, clerks, accountants? Who does your books? Who does your appraisals?

Besides brokers, many other people are involved in real estate, and any one of them can give you some insights into the business. Writers are needed for the ads you see in the newspaper and also for real estate journals. Try to locate a real estate writer by calling your local newspaper office or by writing to the editor of a real estate journal (you can find these journals in the library).

How does a writer decide what things about a house should be described in an ad or journal? Is his writing always objective, or does he give his own opinion about a piece of real estate?

People who work in home improvements can also tell you about real estate—what conveniences are required in what buildings and how much they add to the cost of a building. These people include carpenters, plumbers, electricians, and painters.

To learn about governmental regulation of real estate, go to City Hall and ask for the Titles Department. What is a title? What does a title abstractor do? Look under "Titles" in the Yellow Pages of your telephone directory and visit a title company. You could also go to the County Clerk's office, where deeds and mortgages are recorded, or to various courts to find out what liens and litigations are and what tax liens are and where they are placed against property.

Other people involved in real estate include lawyers, accountants, architects, engineers, and surveyors. It should be interesting to compare their opinions about real estate with those of a real estate broker.

What can you learn at a RESTAURANT?

Have you ever taken a good look around a restaurant and tried to estimate the amount of food being consumed at any given time? If this quantity seems colossal, just multiply it by the number of restaurants in your city, the country, the world, and the hours of the day, and you should have some idea of the vastness of the restaurant business.

The best way to learn about the restaurant business is to take a summer job as a cashier, waiter or waitress, busboy, cook, or dishwasher. Many restaurants, especially those located in tourist areas, need extra help in the summer and are glad to hire energetic young people. Restaurants attached to hotels probably also need extra help in the summer; see "Hotel" in this book to learn about other kinds of services based on tourist trade.

Who orders the food for the restaurant and how does he know what and how much will be required? How is food labeled, inventoried, and stored? (How do the answers to these questions compare with the information given by the truck driver in "Food Distribution Center" in this book?) What does the manager do if he runs out of an item on the menu? What does he do if he has a surplus of something?

The chef is another person with a lot of responsibilities and a lot of worries. What does he think would be the worst disaster that could occur in his kitchen? What if one of his reliable recipes unaccountably fails? How far in advance does the chef start preparing? His pots are probably the largest you have ever seen. Where does he get them? What about his electrical appliances? Are they like those in your home? Find out what led him into the field and where he learned his trade. Did you catch what he said about the highly touted French chefs?

Discover the world of the waiter or waitress—the cast of customers, their tipping habits, the tired feet and back, the power of a union. As you deal with the maitre d', you learn to appreciate his power to confer good and bad table locations and to orchestrate the movements of the patrons and staff. At the same time, you admire the bartender who can mix any drink ordered, and you realize that his long bar makes the difference between high and low profits for the restaurant each day. And, with the owner, you have learned to worry when business is slow.

On a slow day, flatter the owner by asking about how he got started. Was it a family legacy or was it KP in the army? What prompted him to buy at the time and location that he did? How do he and the chef decide what to serve? What determines price? In what quantities does he buy silver and tableware? What problems does he have with the laundry service for cloths and linen napkins? Is he dreading the next time he has to lock horns with the union? Has he ever had a food poisoning scare? How does he make sure that health department requirements are met?

If the restaurant has a wine cellar, visit it with the wine steward and ask him about the number of bottles, the age of the oldest bottle, and the grades and kinds of wine he keeps stocked for the clientele of this restaurant.

What can you learn about ROAD BUILDING AND REPAIRING?

I met Ben when I stopped to watch a new street being made near my home. He seemed to be the crew foreman, and I asked him many questions. The construction of the street was an intriguing and complicated process to watch.

Ben explained the step-by-step process of surveying, laying out the roadway, scraping, grading, putting in curbs, and paving. I learned what each of the big pieces of machinery does—the bulldozers, the paving machines, and the steamrollers. After seeing how many steps it takes to build a good street, I did some research at the library to find out how roads got to be the way they are today.

Over the centuries, many different kinds of material have been tried as surfaces for roads. As road traffic has increased steadily over the past seventy-five years,

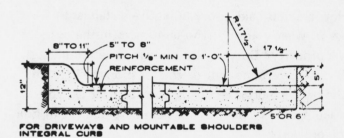

FOR DRIVEWAYS AND MOUNTABLE SHOULDERS
INTEGRAL CURB

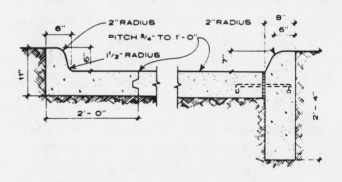

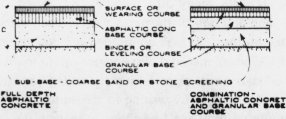

FULL DEPTH ASPHALTIC CONCRETE

COMBINATION - ASPHALTIC CONCRETE AND GRANULAR BASE COURSE

experiments have tested practically all imaginable road surfaces.

In the early 1800s granite blocks were tried in Philadelphia, bricks in Boston, and wooden blocks in New York City. In 1846 a 16-mile road from Syracuse, New York, to Oneida Lake was built out of wooden planks. The cost of that road was $1,487 a mile, which could not pay for five feet of modern roadway in most parts of the country today. A modern road costs upwards of $1,500,000 a mile, with many super-highways costing much more.

At various times, gravel, clay, and even steel and rubber have been tried as road surfaces. The state of Maryland even built a 250-mile road made of oyster shells. Now when I travel around my city I try to find how many different kinds of road surfaces there are. I have found examples of the three basic modern road surfaces—as-phalt, tar, and concrete. Ben explained how each of these materials is made and why it is used in certain situations. Each type of road has its advantages, depend-ing on such things as location, climate, and the amount and type of traffic it must carry. Ben said that the best kind of road has a bituminous concrete surface on a Portland cement concrete base; this gives the great-est strength and carrying capacity with the smoothest ride qualities.

I was lucky enough to become interested in the build-ing of this street early, because I had the opportunity to see all of the utilities that are put underground— water and sewer pipes, gas mains, telephone cables, and electric lines. That made me realize how important streets are for purposes other than just transportation.

Ben also explained how streets get damaged by differ-ent kinds of weather conditions, by the salt that is put down in winter, by studded snow tires and chains, and by normal wear and tear. Each of these culprits leaves its characteristic scars on streets and roads, and different kinds of damage require different kinds of repair work. Ben told me that a typical city spends one-fifth of all its capital funds on building and maintaining streets and related projects, like bridges and highways. That's a lot of money for something that we take for granted.

Now when I'm going someplace and I see a sign that says, "DETOUR. ROAD WORK AHEAD," the possible inconvenience doesn't bother me any more. What the sign actually reads for me is, "LEARNING OPPORTUN-ITY! ROAD WORK AHEAD."

What can you learn from a SOCIAL WORKER?

If you are interested in social problems—like poverty; unemployment; illness; antisocial behavior; broken homes; physical, mental, and emotional handicaps; racial tensions; inadequate medical care; lack of recrea-tional, cultural, and educational opportunities—contact a social worker. A social worker can direct you to those who are also working with these problems, for example, doctors, nurses, nutritionists, city planners, recreation workers, teachers, policemen, and many others.

More than 60 percent of social workers are employed by state, county, and city government agencies, and about 3 percent work for the federal government. Most of the remainder are in voluntary or private agencies. The kind of social work a person does generally de-termines where he is employed. Two categories of social work are casework, which deals directly with individuals or families, and group work, which involves community organizations.

Here is a listing of the different kinds of social workers, where you can find them, and some questions you might ask them about their work:

Public assistance workers: Call information in your telephone directory for state or local public welfare agencies. How do you determine the need for financial assistance? Are there special laws governing amounts of money that can be given to the disabled, blind, aged, unemployed? How do you help clients become self-sufficient?

Family service workers: They can be found in pri-vate agencies. Look in the telephone book, call a cler-gyman for religiously affiliated organizations, or call the Human Services Department at City Hall for in-formation. How do you attempt to improve interper-sonal relations? How do you strengthen family life?

Child welfare workers: They are in government and voluntary agencies that deal with problems of children. What constitutes child abuse? How do you determine who goes into a foster home? How do you find foster homes? Who can adopt children? Are laws for adoption different in different states? Are there some services for families with children when a parent is ill?

School social workers: They are employed through the school system, and you can find them by calling the Board of Education in your town or city. What do you do with the overly aggressive child in school? How do you find out why a child is truant? What relationship do you have with parents, doctors, the principal, truant officers?

Medical social workers: They can be found at hospitals, clinics, health agencies, rehabilitation centers, and also public welfare agencies. What do you do to make sick people more confident about returning from the hospital to the community? How do you help grieving parents after the death of their child? How do you help families of disabled persons cope with their problems? What is your relationship with therapists, doctors, nurses?

Psychiatric social workers: They are employed by mental hospitals and clinics. Can mental illness be prevented? How? What kinds of mental health programs are there in your community? What is the difference between you and a psychiatrist and a psychologist?

Social workers in rehabilitation services: What kinds of problems might a recently handicapped person have when he returns home from the hospital? What are physical and occupational therapists?

Probation and parole officers: They are employed primarily by federal, state, county, and city governments. What kind of investigations do you submit to the court? How do you keep a watch on your client's conduct? Do you have anything to do with child placement and adoption? Are you involved in marriage counseling?

Social group workers: They are employed by settlements and community centers; youth-serving groups; public housing developments; correctional institutions; resident and day-care centers for children, adolescents, or elderly people; and many psychiatric clinics and hospitals. How does a group session work? What are different leadership styles? What kinds of activities might a group participate in?

Community organization workers: They can be found working for welfare agencies, community chests, religious federations, and health associations. What are different methods of fund raising? How do you coordinate existing social services?

What can you learn at a SPORTS STADIUM?

I am a sports stadium. When I am set up for football, I can seat 65,000 spectators; for a baseball game I can accommodate 56,371 fans. Although I may be slightly larger than some other stadiums, I am very much like most of my cousins located in cities throughout the United States. I am a relatively new addition to the family, and I cost over $50 million to build.

I am very versatile. I am mainly used for football or baseball, but I can as easily accommodate a thrill show, a concert, religious services and pageants, field and track events, or soccer, field hockey, rugby, or polo games. Actually, there are virtually no sports events that cannot be held in me. You should visit me sometime during the week and watch my grounds crew prepare me for an upcoming event.

I am located on a 74-acre site, of which almost 60 acres are for automobile parking. When you visit me, you should notice the many design features that have been provided in order to move large numbers of automobiles and tremendous crowds with as much efficiency as possible. You know, there are very few places in the world besides sports stadiums where so many people arrive or leave in such a short period of time and do it so often during the year.

I have 8 ramps, 15 escalators, and 4 elevators. I need 8 large entrance gates and 40 ticket windows. In addition, I possess 60 concession stands and 31 men's rooms and an equal number for ladies.

It would be interesting for you to talk to my managers to find out many things about me, for example: how many people are required to maintain me; how they clean me after a sports event; how ticket sales are operated; how schedules are kept and cleared in advance; what provisions have been made inside me for press, radio, and television coverage; where visiting teams change and keep their equipment; what emergency provisions are made during sports events; how much electricity is required to light my almost 2,000 lights; and what types of special equipment are used to keep me in shape. There's a lot more to learn about me, too.

What can you learn from a TAXICAB DRIVER?

I think you can learn more from a taxicab driver about a city than from anyone else. Talk to a cab driver long enough, and you'll find out about where things are, about feelings of fear and delight, about police, and about new buildings and complexes being built. Some cities have more cabs in them than others, and in these cities it is easier to find a taxicab driver to talk to about his business and about his day. If the cabs in your city are organized into a large company, you can learn a lot by telephoning the public relations office and speaking with the person there. His job is to answer questions from the public. I telephoned the public relations man and spoke with several cab drivers.

In the city of Philadelphia, with a population of two million people, there are 1,100 cabs organized into a company and another 125 independent cabs. Between 400 and 500 of these company cabs have radios. There are over 100 people working in the telephone department taking calls and dispatching them to the cabs with radios.

The taxi fares are set by the Public Utilities Commission. The beginning company driver gets 45 percent of the fare, and after he has worked a while he gets 48 percent. A man working for the company works nine hours a day, including meal time, five days in the summer and six days in the winter. He keeps a sheet recording all the fares, or passengers, he picks up, where he picks them up, and the time, location, and destination of each fare. The Philadelphia cab driver has eight garages to go to in the event that his cab breaks down. The company owns all the cabs and buys new ones when needed.

In order to become a cab driver you must have a driver's license. Then you are trained in safety at one of the company locations and given tests on the state's driving laws. There are street supervisors employed by the company who are out on the streets watching their cabs to make sure rules are not violated. Cab drivers are subject to the same laws as everyone else on the highways. In Philadelphia cab drivers are allowed to go anywhere inside or outside the city, but other cities have other rules. Cab drivers in Philadelphia are not allowed to deliver packages, since another company has this business, but in New Jersey they are. What about the taxicab drivers in your city?

What can you learn from a TEACHER?

Teacher X: "Kids think teachers get locked up in the closet at night and let out in the morning. We're not people to them—we're fixtures in this wreck of a school building. So they treat us like fixtures, and we don't get much of a chance to relate to them as people. I was a lousy student myself, and I figure I've got something to offer kids. I remember the teachers I hated and the dumb assignments I had to do. I want to be the kind of teacher I wish I'd had. I want my kids to have fun learning, and I want to relate to them as one person to another."

Teacher Y: "Students today expect the teacher to let down all the barriers. They don't know what discipline is; they don't know how to finish something they start; they have no respect for anyone older who might just have learned a thing or two over the years. I remember when children knew how to behave—when a teacher could teach. It's not that I hate my students—even though they think I do. It's just that I'm a little at a loss as to how to get through to them. Things have changed so."

Teacher Z: "See, I really love my subject. That's why I went into teaching—so I could continue to read and study. I guess you could say I have something of a problem, in that I'm more involved in *what* I teach than *whom*. Come to think of it, my students probably find me somewhat dull. I mean, you have to get to know people before you can like them. I'd like to know my students better; I really would."

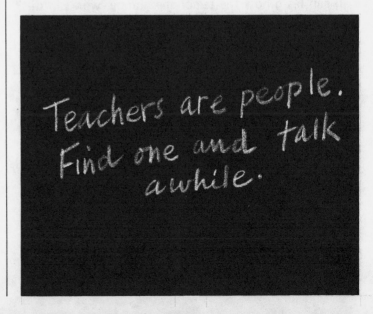

Teachers are people. Find one and talk awhile.

What can you learn about a TELEPHONE?

Can you imagine how our lives would change if suddenly there were no telephones? When you stop to consider it, you begin to realize how dependent we have become on telephones. If you visit the central telephone company office in your city, you can learn how the telephone instrument that you have in your home works. That is the beginning.

At the central office, you can see how the cables run from your house to the central office and how, if there is more than one central office in your city, they are linked together by trunk cables. You will see how the wires lead into giant frames that contain switching mechanisms. These are exposed for servicing and repairs. You will see the generators and the equipment required to convert electrical energy from the electric company into energy for transmitting phone conversations.

You can visit the various departments of the telephone company and see how bills are prepared, how service and repairs are ordered and dispatched, and how operators serve to direct the phone traffic that cannot be dialed directly. Find out how services like weather reports and time information operate. Ask how the telephone directories are compiled. Find out how telephone credit cards work and how long distance bills are prepared. You can find out what happens to the coins from pay telephones and how the operator knows how much money has been deposited in them.

You can learn how the telephone number works in directing the phone call to its proper destination. What role does the telephone exchange (the first three digits) play? You can also learn how area codes make telephone dialing more efficient. And you can see the various designs that have changed the telephone instrument over time and expanded its use.

You can learn how, in a short time, picture phones will be widely used not only to transmit voices but also to convey television images of the speakers. Perhaps you can even see a picture phone demonstrated. You can see how facsimile duplicators can transmit copies of written or printed documents over telephone lines and how television programs as well are transmitted over great distances via telephone lines.

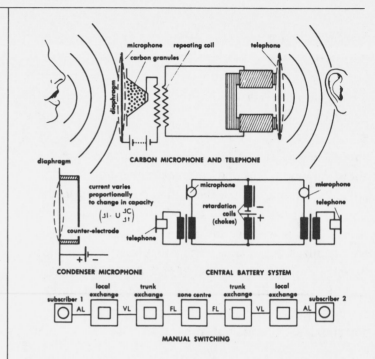

What can you learn from a TELEVISION REPAIRMAN?

There are many skilled repairmen who fix things around the house, like telephones, washing machines, heaters, and other household appliances. Doctors may be making house calls less frequently, but many appliance repairmen still work this way, and most can be valuable learning resources.

Take a television repairman, for example. Ask him how he locates what is wrong with the television set. Find out how he traces the cause of the problem. In a sense he is doing detective work. What kinds of test equipment does he have? How does his test equipment work? What does he test for?

What special tools does he have? How does he store his tools and supplies for easy finding in the truck? What precautions must he take to keep tools and replacement parts from being damaged? How does he work in those hard-to-get-at places inside the television set? How does he adjust a television set from behind without being able to view the screen?

Ask the television repairman to explain how the television set works. Find out how the antenna functions, what a picture tube is, and by what means it reproduces the picture. What are the most common television ailments? What sorts of things cause temporary interference in television reception? Why? What makes the color in color television? How do television cameras work?

How long does the average television set last? Are color television sets harder to fix than black-and-white ones?

Find out how and where the television repairman learned his skills. What made him interested in this type of work? Does he continue his learning and training? What new and better techniques have evolved since he first learned his skills? Where could you go to learn more about televisions, if you are interested? Find out what books and manuals he refers to when he has a problem he cannot solve. Get him to show you how to understand the symbols in a circuit diagram. Ask him what information manufacturers make available about their products in order to facilitate their servicing and repair. Where and how do they make this information available?

Usually, repairmen have developed special ways of working that enable them to do their job faster and more easily. Work habits are very important. When you are not asking questions, stand back and just watch the repairman work. Perhaps you will see patterns, for example, the way he will usually put one tool away before taking out another. He does this so that his tools will always be where he can find them easily. Also, watch how he stores and labels spare parts and small tools for easy access. Does he carry any tools in his pockets? Why?

Next time the television set breaks, do not despair. Look forward to the opportunity to learn from the television repairman. And, you can feel that you have gotten more for your money when you pay the repair bill. Remember, too, that you can learn from any other kind of repairman in the same way.

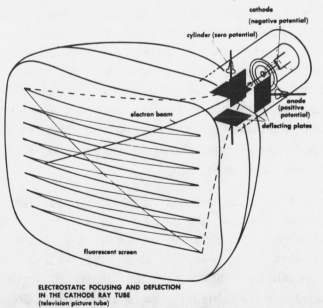

ELECTROSTATIC FOCUSING AND DEFLECTION IN THE CATHODE RAY TUBE (television picture tube)

What can you learn at a TELEVISION STATION?

The best way to learn about a television station is to take a tour or attend a rehearsal or taping of a show. Arrangements can generally be made through the public relations or community relations office of a television station. As you walk around, look at the activities going on and notice the kinds of experts involved and what they do. Write down questions as you tour and then ask the tour guide for answers or the name of a person who could answer them for you.

Here are *some* of the people who put on a television program. Who are these people and what do they do?

1. Producers
2. Script directors
3. Show directors
4. Scenery and set designers
5. Unit managers
6. Technical directors
7. Carpenters
8. Painters
9. Truck drivers
10. Actors and actresses
11. Dancers and singers
12. Costume designers
13. Wardrobe ladies and seamstresses
14. Electricians
15. Prop people
16. Printers
17. Makeup artists
18. Special effects men
19. Cameramen
20. Boom man
21. Lighting engineer
22. Stage manager
23. Video or picture engineer
24. Film librarian
25. Darkroom specialist
26. Writers
27. Reporters
28. News commentators
29. Publicity photographers
30. Camera repairmen
31. Clerical staff
32. Public relations personnel
33. Ushers
34. Telephone operators
35. Accountants
36. Purchasers
37. Time salesmen
38. Sales manager
39. Statistical clerks
40. Researchers
41. Personnel workers
42. Announcer
43. Newscaster
44. Film editors
45. Broadcast technician
46. Development engineers

Who decides which shows will be produced? Who decides when they will be aired? Who writes the script? Who chooses the script? How much space is needed for a scene? How do you replicate a forest indoors? What do you do when there are several scenes with different sets but only one space to work in? Who builds special furniture? Who keeps a record of what "property" the station owns? Are there certain colors that must be used for costumes and sets?

Who figures out the budget? Who determines where financial cuts are to be made? How much does a studio rent for? Who hires the cast? Does a television station have its own cast or are people hired from outside? How are the credits printed?

How does a cameraman know what to shoot and when to do it? What is the control room? What kind of training does someone need to work in the control room? How are special effects done? Are there laws governing special effects in a studio? How does a television camera work? (See "Photography" in this book.) How many cameras are needed to present a show? How does a television company switch from one show to another at the end of a program? What are the differences among a taped, filmed, and live show? What are the advantages and disadvantages of each type? Where are the video tapes from old shows kept? How do we get filmed news from Moscow or London the same day the events happen? What is remote pick-up? What is closed-circuit television? How is color transmitted?

If there are no commercial television stations near you, try a local college for their closed-circuit operation. Although this will not be nearly so extensive as a commercial television operation, there is still a lot to learn there.

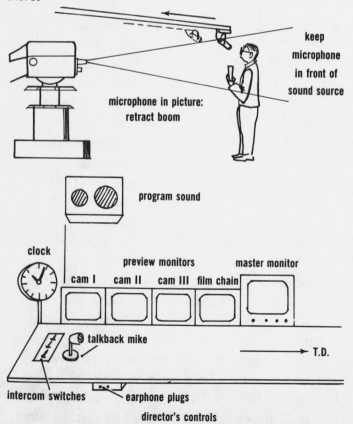

What can you learn about THEATER PRODUCTION?

I really enjoy going to the theater and watching live stage plays. Movies and television are fun, too, but there's an added dimension of excitment when you're watching a live performance. I guess it's the sense of presence—the feeling of really being a part of what's happening on the stage. Most everything is better when it's real and live. Anyway, I always wondered about the many parts that go into making a successful theatrical performance. So one morning I looked up a theater in the Yellow Pages where I had attended a performance two weeks earlier. I called and asked to speak to the manager. I was soon talking to Mrs. Gillmore.

I told her that I was very eager to go behind the scenes of a theater and learn how a performance is put together. Mrs. Gillmore explained that it wasn't normal policy, but she couldn't think of any reason why I couldn't come to visit. She told me to come by that Thursday afternoon, since there would be a dress rehearsal and that would be particularly interesting. You know, I am always amazed at how many normally inaccessible doors you can unlock just by expressing interest and asking to be shown around.

When I arrived, I was directed to Mrs. Gillmore's office and we were introduced. While we spoke, she answered several phone calls and spoke to several people who came into her office. She is a very busy lady. The manager of a theater has to be a jack-of-all-trades. That afternoon Mrs. Gillmore was writing copy for newspaper ads, directing workmen who were renovating parts of the theater, settling tiffs between angry actors and directors, trying to find a lost crate of scenery, and talking to me all at the same time. I found out that Mrs. Gillmore had been an actress and had directed several plays before becoming assistant manager, then manager, of the theater. She said that once you're bitten by the theater bug, you can never get it out of your blood, and she explained that she was a theater person through and through.

I was taken downstairs and ushered backstage. There I met the electrician, who gave me a ten-minute dissertation on the ins and outs of theater lighting. I learned that there are many special types of lights—each offering the possibility of different effects. Colored gels can be placed over the lights for color or mood effects. Some lights are high in front of the stage, some directly over it, and others, called footlights, are in the stage itself at the very front. I saw the control panel where all of these lights are manually switched on and off and phased in and out.

The clamor of activity everywhere around us made it hard for me to believe that people could actually be getting work done, but everyone seemed to know what he was supposed to do. There were more people behind the scenes than there were actors and actresses, but this particular play had a cast of only nine people. Actors were walking around the stage, and I was shown the little marks of tape on the floor that indicate where they should stand for particular scenes. They refer to the process of getting familiar with the stage before a performance as "walking the boards."

I saw the makeup artist at work and was amazed by the array of tools and equipment he had in his kit. Most of the performers put on their own makeup, but the stars must submit to the skilled hand of the makeup artist. It was really fun to see a young actress become a grandmother before my very eyes. The makeup is very stark and dramatic up close, but that is necessary in order to achieve the proper effect for the audience.

The sets were made of canvas stretched across wooden frames, very much like large paintings. Special props hold them up, and bags of sand are used to stabilize them. On stage, many of the sets are exaggerated and out of perspective, but again, that is necessary for the right effect to be visible from the house seats. I saw where old sets are stored and the shop where special sets are built and old ones repainted and remade. In the props room hundreds of different kinds of props —tables, chairs, iron railings, telephones, guns, lamps, and others—are stored.

Mrs. Gillmore invited me to watch the dress rehearsal from the wings, which proved to be a great opportunity. I saw how the stagehands raise and lower the curtain and manipulate the scenery. For many of the scene changes, the lights would go out and the stage hands would walk on stage, unseen by the audience, and instantly transform the set. There are little pieces of fluorescent tape put on the stage to direct their activities in total darkness. The behind-the-scenes work is as well choreographed as the actual performance. The stage manager is in charge, and he is responsible for

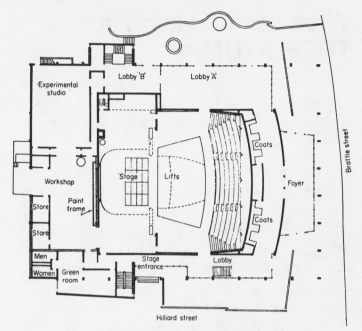

THE LOEB THEATRE, HARVARD UNIVERSITY GROUND FLOOR PLAN

making sure that everyone gets the proper cues. He wears an operator's headset and is linked to the lighting man, one of the stagehands, and the other side of the stage by an intercom system. He is extremely tense during the performance but becomes much more relaxed after the show is over.

After the performance, Mrs. Gillmore introduced me to the cast. I had been too busy watching the technical aspects of the performance to become involved in the play itself. I asked the actors and actresses many questions and found their replies very interesting. It's especially nice to find out how real they are as people. They invited me back to see the opening performance, and I was anxious to see the whole play after seeing all of the separate parts that went into it. I think it was the best time I ever had at the theater, because I was able to appreciate everything a great deal more with the knowledge of the hard work and detailed attention paid to every nuance of the performance. The reality of the live performance comes from more than the fact that real people are acting; every part of **the performance** is artfully arranged to convey a complete and believable experience.

If you are interested in visiting a theater, you can have an exciting afternoon. If there are no theaters near you, you might look for a summer stock company that may be touring in your area. Often, too, amateur theater groups and universities put on excellent plays and will be as interesting to learn from as a professional company.

What can you learn from a TREE STUMP?

Usually, the first thing you notice about a tree stump is its rings. Each ring represents one year's growth, and you can easily tell a tree's age by counting the rings. Try it.

You may be interested in using the tree stump as a means for learning other things as well. For example, you can learn to identify different kinds of trees by their wood. Talk to a man at a lumberyard, a tree surgeon or gardener, a botanist, a boy scout or girl scout, a horticulturist, or a friend who is knowledgeable about nature. You can also learn how archaeologists use trees and logs to date previous settlements. The technique is called "dendrochronology," and it has proved to be a very reliable tool for giving precise dates to archaeological finds. Talk to an archaeologist, an anthropologist, a scientist, or a museum curator, or consult the encyclopedia.

Yes, even a tree stump can be a learning resource.

This tree is 62 years old. It's been through fire and drought, plague and plenty. And all of this is recorded in its rings.

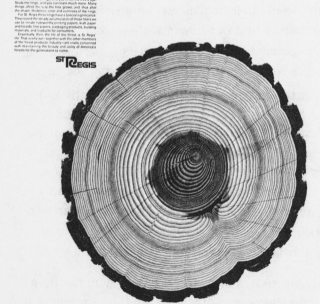

What can you learn from a UNION BOSS?

Unions are such a complex and pervasive part of our economic and social system that it would be impossible to deal with them at any length here. In a way, unionism is as big a subject as our government—and as multifaceted. Union membership affects not only a person's work and salary, but also his health, old age, vacations, and recreation. Two of the most powerful unions in the United States are the United Automobile Workers Union (UAW) and the American Federation of Labor-Congress of Industrial Organizations (AFL-CIO). Within each of these unions, there are many smaller unions. Almost all of the individually performed crafts are organized into unions; in this book, see "Bricklayer," "Carpenter," "Electrician," and "Locksmith."

You can get the name of a union boss, shop steward, or other high-ranking union official by calling the employee relations department of any large factory. Try to get an interview with a union official or union member during his lunch hour or after work and ask him about the following subjects: the definition of a union, the history of unions, legal rights of union members, union fees, hierarchy of authority in the union, different kinds of unions, the difference between an "open" and a "closed" shop, strikes, wage-price spiral, working conditions, retirement, health plans, advancement in the union, race relations in the union, union music, union folklore, automation, child labor, labor laws, the union's relationship to the United States Department of Labor, the union's place in a capitalistic society, unionism in other countries.

Why did he join the union? What benefits does he receive? Are there any disadvantages to belonging to a union? In what direction does he see his union moving? Is he in favor of the four-day week? What is his opinion of individual union bosses or other officials? Does he personally get involved in collective bargaining? What is his preferred strategy of bargaining? How would he describe the relationship between unions and management in his particular company?

What can you learn from an UPHOLSTERER?

"It's harder to buy a chair than to buy a car," claims one of the leading manufacturers of furniture.

Perhaps if you have seen someone pick a print fabric to cover a chair, then switch to a solid color, then vacillate between a wide and narrow stripe, then mumble something about returning tomorrow to decide, you may believe the manufacturer's statement. Your car, he says, does not have to harmonize with other cars on the road, or go with the color scheme in your garage, or complement your shrubbery when it's parked in your driveway. Your chair, on the other hand, must be the right size and have the right fabric. And the fabric must be in the right color or it simply won't look good in your house.

Probably you have never considered what went into making your favorite chair so comfortable. Let the manufacturer tell you about the chair being engineered to the body through the use of strong coils where the weight is concentrated and softer coils where the weight is less. Ask him about the eight-way knotting that keeps the springs springing, not wobbling. He would no doubt also be able to answer your questions about the type of wood used for the frame. Is it seasoned, kiln-dried hardwood that eliminates any chance of warping? Another important fact to check is whether the fabrics used are protected with a stain-repellent finish. Actually, the best person to ply with these questions is the man behind the scenes who really knows the work that goes into making a chair comfortable—the upholsterer.

In addition to working for furniture manufacturers, the furniture upholsterer can be employed in small upholstery shops, furniture stores, and businesses like motels, movie theaters, and hotels that maintain their own furniture. He may also be found at vocational schools, high schools, night schools, or YMCAs. An entirely different branch of the upholstery business comprises those individuals who work as automobile upholsterers or automobile trimmers and installation men.

An upholsterer can teach you about the structure of a piece of furniture and the kind of padding and fabric it needs. He may show you how to replace worn furni-

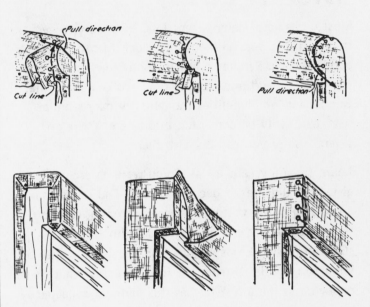

ture fabric, repair broken frames, and replace and repair webbing, bent springs, and other worn parts of furniture. He can show you the variety of hand tools he uses—staple removers, pliers, shears, webbing stretchers, upholstery needles, and hammers. The upholsterer may also lay out his own pattern and cut his fabric with hand shears or a cutting machine.

If the upholsterer is in a small shop, he probably operates his own sewing machine. If not, he can introduce you to the seamstress who can show you how to operate it. Also, the person in a small shop may order his own supplies, keep his own records, and perform other managerial tasks. His operation is similar to other small businesses, and you can learn about taxes, overhead, purchasing, hiring, and record keeping. The small businessman may also do his own delivering.

The upholsterer may be able to introduce you to interior designers and salesmen. He may, from his own experience, tell you about changing tastes in style, improved quality of fabrics, different techniques of webbing, changes in amount of orders, and the effects of changing costs of material and labor.

To locate an upholsterer, look in the Yellow Pages under "Upholsterers"—or find out just where that chair you're sitting in came from! There's sure to be an upholsterer behind it somewhere.

What can you learn at a VACANT LOT?

Most cities have many vacant lots. Invariably, they stick out like missing teeth in a block of otherwise good housing. People complain about the hazards and the ugliness, and most of the time nothing gets done. But vacant lots, liabilities though they may seem at first, can easily be converted into assets. There are several things you can do with them:

Learn from a vacant lot as if you were an archaeologist. How did the lot become vacant? Did it ever have a building on it? If it was never built upon, can you figure out why it was an undesirable lot for construction? What kinds of junk and debris have piled up? What can you learn from the junk and trash that have collected in the lot? Why has this material collected here? What could you reconstruct about the culture of the people who lived around the lot, based only on the things you find on the property? Can you find out who owns the property by going to City Hall and consulting the deed records?

Clean up a vacant lot as a service to your neighborhood. Call City Hall and find out how you can get help in cleaning up the lot. Start with the City Planning Commission or Board; next ask the Health Department. Can the city require the owner to clean up the lot, or will the city undertake the task itself? If worse comes to worst, find out if the city will cart away the debris if you and your friends agree to clean it up. Get a group of people together to help you.

Make a vacant lot into a useful space for your community. There are many governmental programs available to improve vacant lots throughout the city. Call City Hall and consult the City Planning Department or the Redevelopment Agency. Money is sometimes available to convert vacant lots into new housing, playgrounds, parking lots, or parks. Find out if your city has such funds available. Even if there is no money through a governmental program, see if you can get the owner to dedicate the land for community use (even temporarily). Often you will be able to get people to donate materials to fix the lot up. Or you can employ ingenuity to convert inexpensive or unwanted materials into outdoor equipment. For example, old telephone company wire spools, telephone poles, and railroad ties make great playground equipment. Maybe neighbors will contribute their time or money.

Use a vacant lot as an added amenity in your neighborhood—a sort of neighborhood commons. Play there, wash cars there, meet friends there, put up basketball hoops, grow vegetables, have block parties, plant trees and flowers, put up fences, provide benches, make a neighborhood bulletin board. However, obtain the permission of the owner before doing anything; otherwise, you will be trespassing.

If you should decide to do any or all of these things, you will have learned a great deal. Do not overlook the lesson; stop and think about what you've learned about how you can understand and change your environment. If you decide to do nothing about the vacant lots that bother you, you will also have learned an important lesson about why nothing happens to make our cities better places: It is often because people like yourself don't have the time or don't care enough to make things happen.

What can you learn about VOTING?

The right to vote for officials of government is one of the most basic elements of a democratic society. Over the years, the process of voting has been modified and refined to make it the most accurate expression possible of individual opinion. Most city halls have an election department or commission listed in the telephone directory under your city or town. These people are concerned exclusively with elections, and they should be able to answer your questions about the entire procedure. To get the best response, try to get in touch with them at a time other than election time. Your local representatives in municipal, state, and national government should also be willing to explain voting to you. Finally, someone in the League of Women Voters, if there is one near you, could also be very helpful in answering your questions about voting.

Here are some things to consider: How has suffrage (the right to vote) been extended over the years? What do the Fifteenth and Nineteenth amendments to the Constitution have to do with voting? What are the residency, age, and literacy requirements for voters? What purpose do they serve? Why must one register to vote? What is a poll tax?

There are over 90,000 units of government—local, state, county, and national—in the United States. How do elections differ according to these levels? Why do we have political parties? What kinds of processes precede final elections, such as nominations, conventions, and primaries?

How does the "one man, one vote" system differ from the electoral college? What is an Australian ballot? How do voting machines work? How are votes counted? When may a candidate demand a recount of votes? How are voting times and places made known to the public?

People who conduct public opinion polls before an election should also be interesting to talk to. Ask them how much of an influence campaigning has on a candidate's success or failure. What are some of the reasons people give for liking a particular candidate? Do these people think that publishing the results of a public opinion poll before an election affects the final outcome?

Finally, remember that this whole complex process has been designed because your opinion is important. If you are old enough to vote, vote!

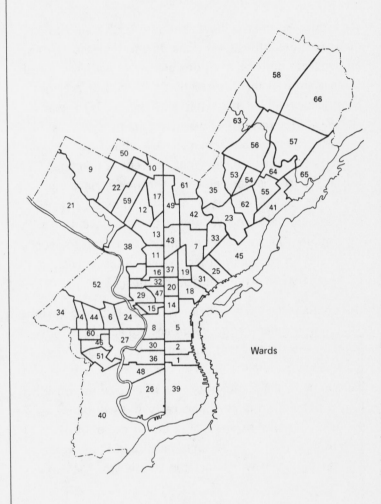

Wards

What can you learn from a WARD LEADER?

Scene: Polling booth
Personages: Politicians
Protagonist: You, the voter

The voter strides into the voting booth and unhesitatingly pulls certain levers. As he leaves, strains of "God Bless America" are heard.

Whom did you vote for? How much of your vote was determined by a desire for good government and how much by the influence of the politicians in your area? There is a good chance that your vote was partially affected by one of the extremely powerful men in politics today—the ward leader. Subtly or blatantly he can influence the vote of the people in your community. If he is for honest government, your city will benefit from his power.

Each city, borough, village, or town is divided into some sort of political divisions. In some places, mostly cities, these political divisions are called wards. In rural areas they are called precincts. Each ward or precinct has a leader elected as the party official; he is the ward leader. All the rewards of working to get the party's candidate elected to a high office will then flow through the ward leader. What happens is that the political party he has helped put in power pays him with jobs, called patronage jobs, which he may distribute around his ward. When you, the voter, went into that polling booth, were you anxious to keep the current party in power in order to save your uncle's job because it stems from political patronage?

Are there special problems in your neighborhood, such as zoning ordinances, poor garbage collection, or potholes in the streets, that are not being remedied? Ideally, it is the job of the ward leader to know what is happening in his community. He should be responsible to the people in his ward and carry the will of the people to the politicians higher up on the political totem pole. At the same time, he should know what is happening that will affect the people who elected him.

How many people know their ward leader's name? How many ward leaders make themselves available to their constituents when a problem arises? The responsible ward leader is accessible to his community. Do you have a problem? Do you want to interview him for your school newspaper or for your political science course? Do you want to work for a political party? Do you want an absentee voting ballot, or are you simply curious about what a ward leader does? You can track him down by phoning City Hall or the county government office building. Also, each political party has a list of ward leaders.

As they grow more interested and involved in politics, many people get hooked. If you find yourself getting hooked by the "pol" scene, there are two books, among many others, you will enjoy: *The Last Hurrah* by Edwin O'Connor, a fiction book about Boston politics, and *Boss* by Mike Royko, a nonfiction account of Mayor Richard Daley's reign in Chicago.

What can you learn about WEATHER FORECASTING?

Don't knock the weather; nine-tenths of the people couldn't start a conversation if it didn't change once in a while.
—Kin Hubbard (American humorist)

The weather is an ever-present part of our environment. We are constantly bombarded with conversation about it, reports in newspapers and on television and radio on the subject, predictions of what it will be, and disappointments over things we can't do because of it. Yet most of us understand very little about what makes the weather and how it can be scientifically forecast.

Learning about weather forecasting, or meteorology, as it is called, can be an exciting way to extend your basic understanding of elementary scientific principles. Besides, it's fun, since you can use what you learn immediately and often.

See if there is a local weather bureau station in your city as a place to begin the process of learning about weather forecasting. It may be listed in the telephone directory under "U.S. Government, Weather Bureau." There may even be private meteorological consultants listed under "Weather Forecast Services" in the Yellow Pages of the telephone directory. If you can't find anything in the telephone book, try the airport. Airports generally have extensive weather forecasting facilities. Also, many science museums have detailed weather exhibits and weather forecasting displays and facilities. There are clubs of local weather forecasting buffs, many of whom assist the U.S. Weather Bureau by contributing information about the weather conditions in their particular locale. If you can establish contact with one of the clubs or its members in your city, you can tap them as a learning resource. Also, many toy and hobby stores sell beginner kits for starting a hobby of weather forecasting in your home. More advanced equipment is also available from suppliers of scientific instruments. You should also visit your local library for books and reference material about weather forecasting. Try the children's department of the library; they have books on the subject that would interest even adults.

Here are some questions about weather and weather forecasting to help you in your learning project:

What makes the weather?
How does the sun affect the earth?
What is meant by atmosphere?
What are the different levels of the earth's atmosphere?
How does the moon affect the earth?
How does the earth's rotation affect weather?

What are clouds?
How are clouds formed?
How do clouds change over time?
What are the characteristics of the following types of clouds?

Cirrus	Cumulus
Cirrostratus	Stratocumulus
Altostratus	Stratus
Altocumulus	Nimbostratus
Cumulonimbus	

What symbols are used to designate these cloud formations?
How do clouds affect weather?

What makes the wind blow?
Where does wind get its force?
What is meant by the term "prevailing winds"?
What is the difference between an air current and wind?
What is meant by the term "convection"?
What is meant by the following wind designations?

Calm	Moderate gale
Light air	Fresh gale
Light breeze	Strong gale
Gentle breeze	Whole gale
Moderate breeze	Storm
Fresh breeze	Hurricane
Strong breeze	

How can you learn to recognize these winds without instruments?
How does wind affect weather?

What is atmospheric pressure?
How much does air weigh?
Why does air weigh different amounts at different altitudes?
How does air pressure affect winds?
How is air pressure measured?
What is meant by high- and low-pressure areas?
How does air pressure affect weather?

What validity do the following weather proverbs have?
"Rainbow to windward, foul falls the day; rainbow to landward, rain runs away."
"Thunder in the morning, rain before night."
"Who soweth in rain shall reap with tears."
"The north wind doth blow, and we shall have snow."
"If wind follows sun, fair weather will come."
"If clouds fight the wind, a storm will begin."
"Rain before seven, lift before eleven."
"Fog from seaward, fair weather; fog from landward, rain."
"When sounds are clear, rain is near."

How are weather phenomena caused?

What causes dew?	What causes fog?
What causes frost?	What causes sleet?
What causes rain?	What causes hail?
What causes snow?	What causes lightning?

What makes the seasons change?
What is meant by hot and cold fronts?

How are weather forecasting instruments used?
How does a thermometer work?
How does a maximum-minimum thermometer record highs and lows?
How do the different types of barometers operate?
How does an anemometer measure wind velocity?
How does a weather vane indicate the direction of the wind?
How does a sling psychrometer work?
How does a rain gauge record precipitation?
How are weather balloons used?
How does radar aid weather forecasting?
How are satellites employed in weather forecasting?

How are weather forecasts prepared?
What information is required to make a scientific weather forecast?
How are weather maps prepared?
What are the standard weather map symbols?
Who prepares weather forecasts at the weather bureau?
How often are the weather forecasters correct?
What happens to make the weather forecast incorrect?
Of what value are weather forecasts?

Can man affect the weather?
Can man make rain?
Can man change the temperature of the outside air?
Can man change wind directions?
Can man avert hurricanes and tornadoes?
Can man prevent snow?
How does air and water pollution affect weather?

What can you learn from an X-RAY TECHNICIAN?

"Happiness is having my technicians work with me year after year," my uncle, a radiologist in a 900-bed hospital, always tells me when he treats me to a visit with him on occasional Saturdays. "Without the highly skilled x-ray technician, this radiology department would not be able to function efficiently."

X-raying is a form of electromagnetic radiation capable of penetrating solids and of ionizing gases. Before Wilhelm Konrad Roentgen (1845-1923) discovered x-rays in 1895, an achievement that won him a Nobel Prize in 1901, the only way to know what was happening in a patient was to cut him open. Pointing to the equipment, my uncle explains that a good technician's working knowledge of anatomy and physiology enables him to position the patient and the x-ray equipment so that the section of the body to be x-rayed is accurately filmed. Equally important, a technician knows the effects of excessive radiation on the body and the necessity of preventing damage through radiation by covering the gonads and blood-producing organs, such as bone marrow, with a protective lead plate.

The range of information a technician must acquire, first through special schooling and then on the job, is so varied that with each visit to the hospital I think of new questions to ask about working with x-rays. To help me learn as much as possible, my uncle sometimes permits me to follow the chief technician through his duties.

Immediately, I notice how considerate the chief technician is when a patient arrives, so that the patient understands what is happening and feels secure instead of frightened. While the patient is given an "opaque" to drink, the technician explains to me that the patient swallows the opaque, which contains barium salts, in order to make certain organs visible on the x-ray.

I question the technician about angiography, a relatively new area of radiology that involves injecting the opaque through thin tubes, called catheters, that are worked by the doctor into the artery that feeds the organ to be x-rayed. Some technicians specialize in this field.

The chief technician makes the x-ray equipment less mysterious as he clears up questions about proper voltage, current, and exposure time. He also explains what happens after the x-ray is taken—how it is developed and how the darkroom chemistry works. Although this chief technician prefers diagnostic radiology, which involves the taking of x-rays for the purpose of making diagnoses, the Radiology Department also contains a therapy section, where technicians work with equipment meant for fighting certain illnesses, such as cancer. Approximately one-quarter of all x-ray technicians work in hospitals along with radiologists, nurses, medical engineers, scientists, and chemists, all involved in aspects of x-raying. The remainder are in smaller institutions, such as medical laboratories, physicians' and dentists' offices, clinics, federal and state agencies, school systems, and even in small mobile units.

In many states technicians must be registered. The American Registry of Radiologic Technologists, 1600 Wayzota Blvd., Minneapolis, Minn. 55405, provides information on registration and careers.

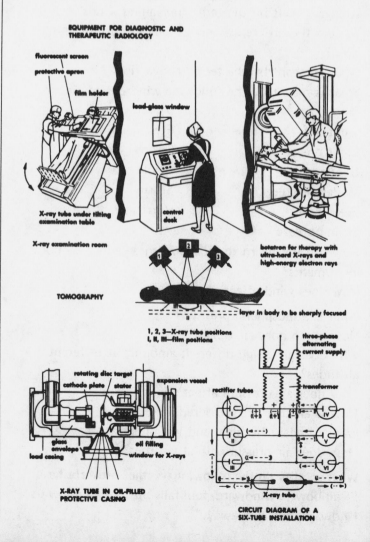

What can you learn from the YELLOW PAGES TELEPHONE DIRECTORY?

If you have read this far, you should not need any convincing about the value of the Yellow Pages telephone directory. For any curious person, it belongs on the shelf right next to the dictionary, the almanac, and the *Whole Earth Catalog*.

As the directory itself tells you in the beginning, you can use it to find (1) a firm if you only know the address, (2) the name of a firm you've forgotten but would recognize, (3) particular brand names or services, and (4) a unique or unusual product or service. In addition, there's often a "Going Places in and around Your City" section. Then there's a collection of valuable postal information, a zip code map for your city, an area code directory, and lots of useful telephone rate and dialing information.

Still, the best information is in the body of the directory itself. There you will find the "who," "what," and "where" of practically everything imaginable in your city (and lots of things you have not even imagined). Besides being a telephone directory, it is a veritable learning resource directory. You can even "window shop" for learning opportunities without having anything particular in mind. You should become familiar with the index in the beginning and learn to use it. Most of the people I have talked to do not even realize it's there. If you are interested in other cities, you can obtain their Yellow Pages directories from your telephone company for a small fee.

I often wonder if there was nothing left of our civilization, say, five hundred years hence, how accurately some talented anthropologists of the twenty-sixth century could reconstruct our culture by using only a copy of the Yellow Pages telephone directory. Perhaps they would also need a Sears Catalog, but I would be willing to bet on the validity of their reconstruction—all the information is there. In fact, when I visit a new city for the first time, I make it a point to flip through their Yellow Pages.

When you come right down to it, the Yellow Pages telephone directory is the best learning resource available to further your ability to utilize the city.

What can you learn about ZONING?

Zoning is a means of regulating the use of land and guiding growth patterns along desired lines in accord with a city's or town's comprehensive plan. Often misunderstood, zoning is most frequently used to keep land from being used in ways that might work against the "public interest."

The legal authority for zoning derives from the "public police power," which has traditionally allowed governments to regulate and restrict individual freedoms when doing so is necessary to protect the public interest. The public police power is the source of authority for other laws, such as those that control vehicle speeds on roads and highways, require children to attend school, and prosecute people guilty of crimes, such as robbery, for example. The power to zone resides with the states but has historically been passed on to municipal governments via enabling legislation.

Consider the following article enunciating a typical zoning ordinance's purposes:

The Zoning regulations and districts hereinafter set forth are made in accord with a comprehensive plan to promote the public health, safety and general welfare, provide for adequate light, air and convenient access, lessen congestion on the streets, secure safety from fire panics and other dangers, prevent overcrowding of the land, avoid undue concentration of population, facilitate adequate provision for transportation, water, sewage, schools, parks and other public requirements by regulating and limiting the height and bulk of buildings, the portion of lot area that may be occupied, the area of yards, courts and other open spaces, and by regulating and restricting the location of trades, industries and buildings designed for specified uses. The regulations are made with reasonable consideration among other things, to the character of each district, its peculiar suitability for particular uses and the directions of building development, and to conserve and encourage the most appropriate use of land throughout the Town.

You can visit the city planning agency in your city to begin your understanding of zoning. Locate your home, and identify the zoning for your neighborhood by examining the zoning maps. Read through your city's zoning ordinance. Attend a meeting of the Zoning Board of Appeals in your city, especially when a motion is before the board concerning a change in your community. Find out how citizens can participate in the process of determining the growth patterns for their communities and what it takes to make a change in the existing zoning ordinance.

Here are some questions you might ask a city planner or a member of the Zoning Board in your city or town:

What is zoning?
What is the purpose of zoning?
How does zoning affect traffic congestion?
How does zoning seek to promote health and welfare?
How does zoning protect citizens from fire, flood, and other hazards?
What is the history of zoning legislation?
What is meant by the term "public police power"?
What is meant by the concept of the "public interest" or "common good"?
How do we reconcile zoning restrictions with our country's heritage of individual property rights?

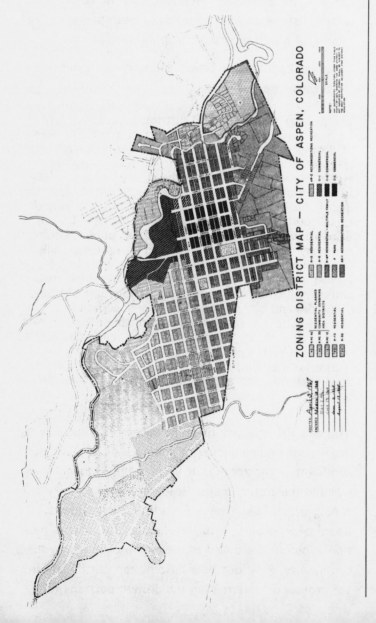

ZONING DISTRICT MAP — CITY OF ASPEN, COLORADO

How is zoning enacted?
Where does the authority for zoning come from?
Who has the power to zone?
What preliminary studies should be prepared before establishing a zoning ordinance?
What is the relationship between a zoning ordinance and a city's Comprehensive Plan?
Who prepares the zoning legislation?
How are the standards developed for the zoning ordinance?
How important is zoning as a tool for planning a city's growth and development?
Can a zoning ordinance be arbitrary or capricious?
How is the inherent suitability of land for certain uses determined?
How do citizens participate in the development of a zoning ordinance?

How does zoning work?
What language is used in zoning ordinances?
What role does precedent play in upholding zoning ordinances?
How is zoning enforced?
How is zoning changed or amended?
Are exceptions to zoning regulations ever made?
What happens if the zoning is changed after uses are already established in the area?
What is a zoning variance?
What is a nonconforming use?
What is the Zoning Board of Adjustment?
What is the Zoning Board of Appeals?
Who selects the members of the zoning boards?
Are zoning cases ever taken into the courts?
On what basis may a zoning designation be disallowed?
How may a zoning ordinance be declared null and void?

How does zoning affect our lives?
What is the zoning for the building we are now sitting in?
How does zoning determine the shape of our cities?
How does zoning determine the appearance of our highways?
How does zoning affect minority groups in our cities?
What are the limitations of zoning?
How could we use zoning more effectively?
Could I participate in zoning decisions?

Read the section "City Planning" in this book.
What part does zoning play in city planning? Does zoning ever work against city planning?

What can you learn at a ZOO?

If you are half as interested in animals as I am, you have probably visited the zoo many times. But, like me, you probably never stopped to consider seriously what it takes to run a zoo. Also, you probably never realized, as I hadn't until recently, how much there is to learn at a zoo.

About a month ago, I called the director of our city's zoo and asked him if it would be possible for me to get a "behind-the-scenes look" at how a zoo operates. I explained my interest in understanding what it takes to run a zoo and in finding out how much I could learn there. He was pleased to assist me in this effort.

On the day I visited the zoo, I first met with the director in his office. He outlined the history of zoos and surprised me by describing zoos that existed in ancient China and Egypt. I hadn't realized that zoos were that old. Next we discussed where the funds come from that support the zoo and how the monies are spent. And, finally, we talked about the staff required to care for the large number of animals housed at the zoological gardens. After about an hour, I was introduced to one of the director's assistants, who guided my tour through many of the zoo's operations. I watched the meat being prepared for the large and small cats, and I saw the many different kinds of food needed for all the other animals. The kitchen looked a lot like what you might expect to find in a large restaurant, although there weren't as many utensils or fancy items.

I visited the veterinary hospital and saw the quarantine cages where animals that have become ill are treated. I spoke with the visiting veterinarian about various animal diseases and about the work being done in the field of animal research. He told me about the problems zoos have in seeking to maintain the natural climatic conditions required to keep the animals healthy. I learned how animal wastes are disposed of and was surprised to discover that there are actually laws that require that certain animal wastes be burned.

I was introduced to several of the keepers and found that they frequently become so attached to their animals that they can predict their behavior patterns by understanding their animals' personalities. You know, to hear the keepers talk, you would think that many of the animals were just like people, and I suppose to their keepers, they really are.

I was very interested in finding out where the animals in the zoo came from. Many zoo animals are captured in their natural habitats, while some are traded with other zoos. One of the dangers that zoo keepers are careful to avoid is the development of what they refer to as a "zoo breed" of a particular species. This problem occurs when zoo animals have bred together for so many generations that the resulting offspring are no longer representative of their wild, or natural, counterparts. Therefore, zoo keepers consider it important to prevent too much in-breeding; they do this by introducing new animals to the genetic stock. I was surprised at the fact that some zoo animals will not reproduce in captivity at all and that other species rarely do it successfully.

The director's assistant explained to me the way the zoo views its role in modern society. In addition to the traditional goal of providing a recreational opportunity for visitors, zoos are increasingly seeking to provide educational services—especially education about conservation and ecology. Zoos have also been responsible for saving several endangered animal species from extinction by engaging in captive propagation. This danger will become even more critical, unless we all begin to take a more active role in

ensuring the protection and conservation of our natural wildlife.

I expressed dislike for the jail-like zoo exhibits I had seen at many zoos, where the animals are kept in small, unimaginative cages. My guide explained that zoos were waking up to the need to replicate natural habitats in their exhibits and to make the confining elements as inconspicuous as possible. He pointed out many of these advanced exhibiting techniques that had been installed in our own zoo as we toured. In addition to using larger exhibit areas, many zoos are starting to exhibit animals in natural habitat groupings, which provide the added excitement of watching animals interact naturally as they would in their native surroundings.

At the end of my visit, I was astounded to learn that one of the very serious problems at the zoo was vandalism. The assistant told me that there was a growing problem of a small number of people who seem to gain some sort of perverse pleasure by throwing dangerous objects at the animals or by feeding them foods that are detrimental to their health. He told me they had lost three valuable animals during the previous year due to this kind of unforgivable mischief and that the security problem was becoming more serious each year. "At one time," he reported, "we were most concerned with protecting people from animals; now we find we have to spend as much energy protecting the animals from people."

How to Use This Book

Learning from an Anonymous Building

Now that you have read how different people, places, and processes—those that are part of your everyday experience—can open new areas of interest and investigation, how do you go about finding these resources?

One place to start is a large office building in your town. Most buildings will have a directory in the lobby, which will list the names of the occupants. Sometimes they will also list a director or superintendent's name. To learn more about an individual company, you can ask an elevator operator for the name of the company's director, talk to the building manager, or walk directly into the superintendent's office.

Whichever office you enter, carry a pencil and paper and be prepared with a basic framework of questions and a concise explanation of whom you want to talk to and why you are there. There will generally be a receptionist as you enter. Ask for the director or manager. If these are inappropriate titles for this company, the receptionist will say so. Then give your name and explain your purpose. The receptionist will give you the name of the proper person; if he or she is not available, make an appointment.

In order to give an example of the breadth of possibilities in one building, a survey of an eleven-story downtown office building in an Eastern city was taken and produced the following list of occupants:

Three finance companies
Real estate broker
Psychologist
Optometrist
Four private lawyers
Public defenders
Four local trade union headquarters
Beauty shop
Shoe store
Tap room
Pizza parlor
Architectural engineers
Bondsmen
Two dentists
Jewelry shop
Two community organizations
Small magazine headquarters

Food concession stand
Collection agency
Wholesale kitchen equipment company
Court reporters
Security guard agency
Two city agencies
Political group
Medical laboratory
Building manager, superintendent, building agent, and other staff
Four insurance agents
Educational organization
Public relations agency
Two accountants
Employment agency

Even if you were to investigate only one-quarter of a list like this, learning all about the company, its personnel, its business, and all of the other kinds of companies and people involved with it, you would learn a great deal about the interlocking of resources and problems in your community.

Guidelines for Group Learning

As you have learned, the education and enjoyment potential of the community is great. But reading about the resources is often quite different from actual investigation. Where do you begin? Must you start with a subject area or can you just start with a city block or a building? There are a few general guidelines that may be helpful to you before you embark on your project.

What is the size of the group? Will this be for your entire group, a portion of it (like five people), or, perhaps, is it for only one individual?

Where will the activity take place? Will you go to the place or the person (to the journalist, airport, street corner, etc.), or will the resource come to you (pharmacist or clergyman come to speak before your community group, class, etc.)?

How long will the relationship between you and the resource last? Will it be a one-day visit to a factory or a two-part tour of a hospital by the whole group followed by once-a-week visits by one or two of the group to spend concentrated time with the financial vice-president and a file clerk at the registration desk, or a two-week all-day involvement with a lawyer?

What is the purpose of the investigation? Do you want to get a general overview of a block in your neighborhood? Do you want to know the relationship of city agencies to your street? Are you interested in vocational opportunities? Do you want to know the relationship of one individual to a whole organization (for example, a marketing executive in a cosmetic firm)?

After you are able to answer the preceding questions, also keep the following guidelines in mind.

The planning of the activity should involve the prospective participants. If you are a teacher or a group leader, your students or group members should help define the project's goals and then define the method of reaching these goals—the searching out of the resources, planning and organizing the resources, participants, and schedule.

All projects should allow for discussion and shared-learning periods. This is particularly true of an extended project. But even if it is a one-time visit and you are taking your child or a brother or sister, you should incorporate a let's-talk-it-over session to reinforce new learning or plan for a follow-up session to clear up uncertainties. The discussion should also include an evaluation of the activity, which will help you to plan better for further projects and to be more sensitive to learning opportunities in both everyday and specially planned activities.

As you plan a project, it is advantageous to start with familiar resources before introducing totally unfamiliar ones. When learning about building and zoning codes, for instance, start with your own home and neighborhood (or that of the group). When you are learning about a hospital, start with a doctor or a nurse, before an accountant or a physical therapist.

An investigation will tend to be more successful if it involves action, not only study. If you are learning about air pollution, learn who the polluters are. It is far more satisfying to plan an action that might involve reporting an offender, publicizing business or government agencies that break pollution laws, or planning and implementing a publicity campaign for your neighborhood, instructing the residents on how to combat pollution.

Because everything in the community is interdisciplinary and interlocked, it is natural to assume that one well-planned project will lead to many more. For example, start anywhere on this diagram and you will see that everything has some relationship to everything else.

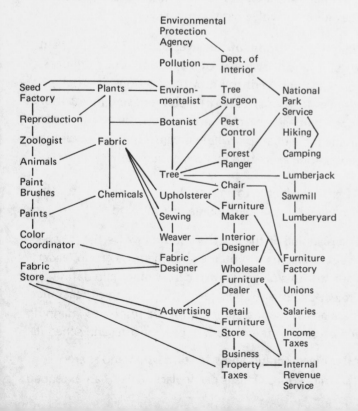

Experimenting in Elementary School

When one thinks of actively learning about the community, one usually thinks of an adult or a teen-ager but rarely sees the elementary-age child as an active participant.

One elementary school decided to experiment. There are thirty-two students between ten and eleven years old in this fifth grade class with one teacher. The teacher made all of the initial arrangements; but as these are proving to be successful, other organizations and people are contacting the school directly.

The students are involved for approximately two to four hours a week. The kinds of activities are varied, giving students a broad range of experiences. Each activity involves approximately two to eight students, depending upon the nature of the activity, where it takes place, and the student selection process. The students are generally walked over to their activity by the teacher or by volunteer college students.

Here is a list of some people, places, and processes these students are investigating:

City Hall. The students go to court hearings and sit in the jury box. The judges will often speak to them directly from the bench to be sure that the students understand what is going on. The students also do a variety of clerical activities under the supervision of someone in the office of the City Council. Everything they do is explained—explained both for skill learning (for example, how to file) and for the reason behind it (for example, these are records of housing complaints). They answer phones, type, file, stamp the city seal, address envelopes, use the Xerox machine and adding machines.

YMCA. The students work in the day care center with one- to three-year-old children. They play games and help care for them.

Political Headquarters. The students do the same kinds of things all political volunteers do. They answer phones, address envelopes, file, and interview the candidates on a regular basis. They also attend many of the local political rallies.

Photography. A photographer volunteers his time several hours a week to work with the students. The students have learned how to use still and moving cameras, how to develop their own film, and how to use film to investigate a subject area, for example, city planning.

Board of Education. The students work with the social

studies department. They do many different kinds of clerical duties, many of which take them all around the building. As a result, they have become very familiar with the different departments and people involved in the education of the public school students. They also interview many of these people, including the superintendent and his associates. While they are working there, they are also given lessons in African history, since the supervisor in charge of the students is an African scholar.

Science Museum. Because the school is located near the city's Science Museum, several students are attached to the education supervisor. Every morning the students set up the apparatus for the day's experiment. The experiments remain the same for a week; by the end of the week, the students know and can explain the entire experiment. One day a week, the students remain for the presentation to visiting groups and act as aides to the demonstrator.

Food Co-op. The students run the register, pack the bags, stamp incoming products, set up displays, and shelve. As an added incentive to a new way of learning mathematics and organization, the students get a free lunch!

Anthropological Museum. Three anthropology students and their professor from a local university have taken a special interest in these students and each week are teaching them about different cultures through the exhibits. The students have also been involved in taking polls in the area to determine why the attendance at this free museum is not higher and are making and distributing posters to encourage more people to visit.

Stock Exchange and Computer Center. Besides the usual tour and clerical duties associated with many of their other activities, the students also learn to work with computers. They learn to read the stock page, select a company to follow, help write a program for the computer, and then try to predict the stock activity of the company. They also learn how to run a small computer.

Once a week the students spend a good part of the day making presentations to the rest of the class about the week's activities. Not only do they talk about their activities, but they also read extra books on their subject area, show their work (for example, one student at the Anthropological Museum is an excellent artist and displays his drawings of the artifacts while explaining what he has learned), and actually teach the rest of the group. While the students are learning, so is the teacher. It is now unnecessary for her to avoid those subject areas she knows nothing or little about. She has the students work with an expert and learn for themselves.

The success of this program has been largely due to excellent organization and planning and an attempt to match a student's interest to a particular activity. Through this program, the students have become more independent, self-reliant, and outgoing. For many students who were having difficulty with basic skills like reading and mathematics, these kinds of experiences have shown them the practical needs for these skills, offered a more exciting way of learning them, and, more importantly, provided the motivation to learn more.

A New Approach to Adult Education

An adult discussion group meets biweekly. They have decided to spend a month or two on urban problems. Previously they had speakers come to their meeting place, but this time they decided to do things differently. This time they wanted to actually go out into the community and learn more directly about the problems and the people involved. They also decided that they would establish some ongoing action-oriented program.

The group established the following procedure: The twelve members split into groups of three, with each group specializing in one of the following areas:
1. Housing
2. Employment
3. Mental health (including drugs and alcohol)
4. Education

The group members attempted to meet people involved in these four areas by making appointments with individuals in various agencies or by doing volunteer work. Where this was not possible, group members did individual research on their particular subjects.

One of the two meetings each month is now devoted to discussion and sharing of learning experiences, while the second continues to involve a speaker, in the field that the previous meeting concentrated on. However, the group members feel that with the background provided by the people who have either worked in or researched a particular area, they can appreciate better the monthly lecture. Many of the group members have also found their work in the community personally rewarding, as well as instructive.

Illustration Credits

Airport
Architectural Record (New York: McGraw-Hill, August 1968), p. 125.

Architect
Richard Saul Wurman, *Various Dwellings Described in a Comparative Manner* (Philadelphia: Joshua Press, 1964).

Automobile
International Automobile Parade (Philadelphia: Chilton Co., 1962), p. 15.
The Way Things Work (New York: Simon & Schuster, 1967).

Bank
Form from The Fidelity Bank, Philadelphia.
Federal Reserve Bank of New York, *Money: Master or Servant?*, p. 127.

Bricklayer
John A. Mulligan, *Handbook of Masonry Construction* (New York: McGraw-Hill, 1942), p. 150.
Charles G. Ramsey and Harold R. Sleeper, *Architectural Graphic Standards* (New York: John Wiley, 1970), p. 79.

Butcher
Irma S. Rombauer and Marion R. Becker, *The Joy of Cooking* (Indianapolis, Ind.: Bobbs-Merrill, 1964), p. 390.

Carpenter
William J. Hornung, *Blueprint Reading* (Englewood Cliffs, N.J.: Prentice-Hall Inc., 1961), p. 71.
Clifford B. Hicks, *Popular Mechanics Do-It-Yourself* (Chicago: Popular Mechanics, 1955), p. 131.

Cemetery
John J. Bodor, *Rubbings and Textures* (New York: Reinhold, 1968), p. 80.

Child
Grid crayon drawing by Eleanor Louise Jones, age 6, 1969.

City Hall
Aspen-Pitkin County League of Women Voters, *Know Your Local Government* (Aspen, Colo., 1970), p. 13.

City Planning
Murphy Levy Wurman, *Wilkes-Barre Community Renewal Program,* 1969, pp. 62-63.

Computer Programmer
Scientific American, *Information* (San Francisco: W.H. Freeman & Co., 1966), p. 25.

Construction Site
Burnham Kelly, *The Prefabrication of Houses* (Cambridge, Mass.: MIT Press, 1951), pp. 260-261.

Corner
Richard Saul Wurman and John Gallery, *Man-Made Philadelphia* (Cambridge, Mass.: MIT Press, 1972), p. 7.

Courtroom
Morris Bloomstein, *Verdict* (New York: Dodd, Mead, 1968), p. 154.

Department Store
Advertisements from the *Boston Sunday Globe,* May 21, 1972.

Electrician
Charles G. Ramsey and Harold R. Sleeper, *Architectural Graphic Standards* (New York: John Wiley, 1970), p. 545.

Garbage Man
Regional Plan Association, *Waste Management* (New York: Regional Plan Association, March 1968), p. 13.

Gas Station
Photo by Peter Hoyt, reproduced in Robert Venturi, Denise Scott Brown, and Steven Izenour, *Learning from Las Vegas* (Cambridge, Mass.: MIT Press, 1972), p. 42.

Greenhouse
Charles G. Ramsey and Harold R. Sleeper, *Architectural Graphic Standards* (New York: John Wiley, 1970), p. 465.

Hardware Store
Clifford B. Hicks, *Popular Mechanics Do-It-Yourself* (Chicago: Popular Mechanics, 1955), pp. 146 and 148.
Charles G. Ramsey and Harold R. Sleeper, *Architectural Graphic Standards* (New York: John Wiley, 1970), pp. 342-343.

Helicopter
The Way Things Work (New York: Simon & Schuster, 1967), p. 560.

Journalist
Page from the *Philadelphia Daily News,* July 27, 1972.

Junk Yard
Richard Saul Wurman and John Gallery, *Man-Made Philadelphia* (Cambridge, Mass.: MIT Press, 1972), p. 33.

Kindergarten Room
Photo by Joel Katz, *Yale Alumni Magazine.*

Library
Philadelphia Free Public Library, *How to Use the Library*, p. 3.

Locksmith
The Way Things Work (New York: Simon & Schuster, 1967), p. 255.

Lumberyard
Illustration by Jack Kunz for advertisements for the St. Regis Paper Co., 1966.

Money
Brochure from the Philadelphia Mint.
F.B. Thomson, *Money in the Computer Age* (New York: Pergamon Press, 1968), pp. 30-31.

Museum
Arthur Lockwood, *Diagrams* (New York: Watson-Guptill, 1969), pp. 127 (from *Observer*) and 132 (from Eric Newton, *European Painting and Sculpture*, Faber and Faber).

Newspaper Plant
Ben Dalgin, *Advertising Production* (New York: McGraw-Hill, 1946), p. 101.

Orchestra Member
The Concise Oxford Dictionary of Music (Oxford, England: Oxford University Press, 1964), p. 412.
Columbia Encyclopedia, 3rd ed., plate 27.

Paper Box Factory
Design and Environment (New York: RC Publications Inc., Fall 1970), p. 24.

Photography
Beaulieu catalog.

Post Office and Postman
Richard Saul Wurman and John Gallery, *Man-Made Philadelphia* (Cambridge, Mass.: MIT Press, 1972), p. 70.

Quarry
Bureau of Mines, U.S. Department of the Interior, reproduced in *Encyclopaedia Britannica,* 1970 ed., s.v. "Quarrying."

Race Track
Results published in *The Philadelphia Inquirer,* May 19, 1972.

Road Building and Repairing
Charles G. Ramsey and Harold R. Sleeper, *Architectural Graphic Standards* (New York: John Wiley, 1970), pp. 474-475.

Telephone
The Way Things Work (New York: Simon & Schuster, 1967), p. 113.

Television Repairman
The Way Things Work (New York: Simon & Schuster, 1967), p. 127.

Television Station
Herbert Zettl, *Television Production Handbook* (Belmont, Cal.: Wadsworth, 1968), pp. 89 and 395.

Theater Production
Stephen Joseph, *New Theatre Forms* (New York: Theatre Arts Books, 1968), p. 98.

Tree Stump
Illustration by Jack Kunz for advertisements by the St. Regis Paper Co., 1967.

Upholsterer
Page Parker and Joseph G. Fornia, *Upholstering at Home* (New York: Grossman, 1951), pp. 143-144.

Voting
Richard Saul Wurman and John Gallery, *Man-Made Philadelphia* (Cambridge, Mass.: MIT Press, 1972), p. 72.

X-ray Technician
The Way Things Work (New York: Simon & Schuster, 1967), p. 438.

Zoning
City of Aspen, Colorado, *Zoning District Map,* 1967.

Zoo
Fred Drimmer, *The Animal Kingdom* (New York: Doubleday, 1954), pp. 138, 637, 594, 606, 210, and 491.

Appendix:
An *Ad Hoc* Survey of Programs That Use People, Places, and Processes as Learning Resources

The following is a partial directory of schools or educational programs that are making direct use of environments other than the classroom as a learning resource and setting.

It is partial in that it is the fruit of conversations with a small number of people with personal knowledge of such programs, of some correspondence, of access to several directories of tangential emphasis, and then of a four-day blitz of nonstop, coast-to-coast telephoning. Because of our own associations, it is partial to programs utilizing the city. For various other reasons, it is dominated by San Francisco, New England, and Philadelphia entries and, further, is partial to those whose phone was not continually busy—or who were not our doing what this book is all about!

It is also partial to pre-"higher education" efforts due to the fact that the country is swarming, for the moment at least, with universities without walls, campus-free colleges, open colleges, free universities, and so forth. From the standpoint of a survey, these programs not only are nearly countless and varied according to each institution but, happily, are tough to characterize because they usually feature student-designed, individual programs. Everybody's got one or is starting one, so just start asking in your area; you'll be amazed at the activity and opportunities available.

The point here, then, is not to provide an exhaustive listing but rather to give an indication of the extent to which people, places, and processes are being utilized by the minority of programs and schools for which the city or the environment in general is not "invisible." This appendix is thus offered as a reference point for your own efforts and only incidentally as the possible start of a more detailed and thorough information exchange and directory, which the 1972 International Design Conference in Aspen may spawn.

Ground rules and a word on the format: Reference to *school* means an entity with the express purpose of providing instruction; *project* means either a nonschool or a multischool program that exists or has existed; and *proposal* refers to any of these that is in the works but has not yet begun operating. Entries are divided two ways—geographically and by the

degree to which we obtained first-hand information. For the number one (1) listings, we spoke to someone directly associated with the program. Number two (2) listings are of programs on which information was obtained but that could not be reached during the four days of phoning; and the third group listed (3) under each section of the country includes references we didn't manage to check out at all—they may not belong here, or they might include the most significant effort of the lot!

East

1 People, Schools, or Projects Contacted

Rochester, New York
SCHOOL WITHOUT WALLS
Contact: Lew Marks, 4 Elton St., Rochester 14607, tel. (716) 271-4010.
Home base: 4 Elton St., a warehouse office
Data: public school, 175 students, grades 9-12, 10 full-time staff
Notes: all classes meeting in the community; alternatives in basic skill mastery a top priority; highlights: Kodak cooperation, tracing process of administration of justice, "gratifying response from people, their pride/pleasure at kids' interest in their jobs, lives."

Hartford, Connecticut
SHANTI SCHOOL
Contact: Gene Mulcahy, 480 Asylum St., Hartford, tel. (203) 522-6191
Home base: 480 Asylum St., a Hartford railroad station
Data: public, 50 students, ages 15-19
Notes: emphasis on school as a community in itself, on what students as people and culture carriers themselves contribute to the learning community; investigates city as organism, complex of systems; has done comparative study of panhandling in New York and Hartford; a regional high school—inner-city, suburban, and rural; will have 72 kids next year.

New York, New York
ELIZABETH SEEGER SCHOOL
Contact: Carol Losee, 165 West 12th St., tel. (212) 255-0322
Home base: 165 West 12th St.
Data: private ($2500/year), 30 students (50 next year), grades 9-12, 4 full-time staff, 8 part-time
Notes: outreach based on kids' special interests (for example, textiles lead to weaving investigation, garment union, museums; social studies lead to tracing legis-

lation, day in Congressman's office, etc.).

Yarmouth, Maine
Project: REEP—REGIONAL ENVIRONMENTAL EDUCATION PROJECT
Contact: Wesley Willink, Intermediate School, Yarmouth
Data: 5,500 students, K-6
Notes: original program at Yarmouth expanded to five Maine communities; K and 1st use immediate school environment, 2nd and 3rd the local neighborhood, 4th and 5th the whole county, 6th grade the entire region; each level considering 12 basic themes—6 emphasizing natural, 6 the man-made.

Boston, Massachusetts
Project: OPEN CITY
Contact: Jim Zien, Children's Museum of Boston, The Jamaicaway, Boston 02130, tel. (617) 522-4800
Data: 50 kids, ages 11-15 (mostly 12 and 13)
Notes: testing multiple processes for dealing with youngsters' lack of mobility in the city; city's transportation system as key to helping children (1) have a citywide visual experience by easily traveling throughout the city, (2) learn what facilities and institutions exist throughout the city that offer educational experiences to young people, and (3) understand how to reach them by means of public transportation; and also to acquaint transportation people with the special needs of, and potentials for, traveling children.

Philadelphia, Pennsylvania
PARKWAY
Contact: Information Officer, Parkway Program, c/o Franklin Institute, 20th St. and Parkway, Philadelphia 19103
Home base: Franklin Institute (although each of four "units" has its own base)
Data: public school, 800 students (divided among the separate units or communities) and expanding, grades 9-12, staff of 8 teachers, 8 interns per unit
Notes: the Christopher Columbus of schools without walls, for which there may be a Lief Erikson, but for all intents and purposes the fountainhead; within the system and meeting standard requirements, yet only about one-half its classes taught by regular staff; utilizes space, service, and personnel of nearly 200 city institutions, organizations, agencies, etc.; curriculum "development" an ongoing process, based upon opportunities and student and staff interests.

Worcester, Massachusetts
THE ALTERNATIVE SCHOOL
(for now)
Contact: Bill Allard, Worcester Public Schools, or Jack Bierworth, School of Education, University of Massachusetts, Amherst—codirectors
Home base: Elizabeth Street School
Data: public, 50 students, grades 10-12, staff: 4 full-time, 3 interns, 3 part-time
Notes: planning school for expanded school without walls

next fall, more comprehensive K-12 effort eventually.

Watertown, Massachusetts
HOME BASE SCHOOL
Contact: John Sakala, 465 Mt. Auburn St., Watertown, tel. (617) 926-3540
Home base: 465 Mt. Auburn St.
Data: public, 100 students, grades 9-12 (25 per grade), core staff of 6
Notes: emphasis on utilization of community's people and places and student planning of town programs; highlight: Experiences in the out-of-school dimension have generated student demand for three Rs tutoring, based upon their discovered need of such.

Belmont, Massachusetts
HABITAT SCHOOL OF ENVIRONMENT
Contact: William Phillips, Director, 10 Juniper Road, Belmont 02178, tel. (617) 489-3887
Home base: 10 Juniper Rd. (many acres)
Data: private ($2100/year), 20 students (usually post-high-school), ages 16-23, regular staff of 5: physicist, ecologist, anthropologist, planner, botanist (if categorized) plus 50 Boston area resource people
Notes: "We are not an alternative school, but provide a complement/supplement... offering practical training in environmental problem solving." One aim is to show that young people need not so much degree programs as opportunities to serve; for example, a Habitat group has become the authority on snow removal. Exhaustive literature search and analysis has led to expert testimony before environmental engineers, industry, and public officials alike. The biggest payoff?—first time for several students that an effort of theirs has been valued.

Washington, D.C.
SCHOOL WITHOUT WALLS
Contact: Patricia Goins, Principal, 1411 K St. N.W., Washington 20005, tel. (202) 737-4007
Home base: 1411 K St., 12th floor
Data: public, 150 students, grades 9-12, 5 full-time staff, 15 part-time
Notes: somewhat more structured version of Parkway and Metro models; intends to become K-12.

Washington, D.C.
HARVARD STREET SCHOOL
Contact: Molly Barnes, 1752 Swan St. N.W., Washington, tel. (202) 332-2064
Home base: Old Souls Unitarian Church, tel. (202) 234-5097
Data: private (cooperative parent-teacher sliding scale tuition)
Notes: use of Washington and Baltimore institutions, facilities, etc.; use of film and environmental topics; has access to West Virginia farm as country site; comparative study of recycling, living and growing things.

Tunbridge, Vermont, and Boston, Massachusetts
Proposal: TUNBRIDGE SCHOOL
Contact: Jan Rakoff, Director, P.O. Box 85, Harvard Sq. Station, tel. (617) 495-5526

Home base: Tunbridge, Vermont, and a Boston base not yet established
Data: private, 100 students, ages 16-20
Notes: largely student-designed program stressing educational experience outside the classroom, particularly, free vocational exploration and interaction with a wide variety of adults; now have their people in task forces for translating theory into practice; will be working on Tunbridge site during summer; school itself opening July 1973.

Philadelphia, Pennsylvania
Project: PHILADELPHIA URBAN SEMESTER GLCA
Contact: Great Lakes College Association, 59 W. Chelten Ave., Germantown, Philadelphia, tel. (215) VI9-0195
Data: 60-100 students, college undergraduates
Notes: 11 colleges contributing students who study and work with community agencies or schools for a 10-week term or a 16-week semester.

Philadelphia, Pennsylvania
ALTERNATIVES WEST
ALTERNATIVES EAST
Contact: Alan Glatthorn, Director
Home base: East—1375 Ashbourne Rd., Elkins Park, Pa.
West—410 Montgomery Ave., Wynnewood, Pa.
Data: public, 171 students at East, 117 at West
Notes: experimental program providing smaller, less structured program; feature of note for us is requirement of 6 hours per week of community outreach activity; largely suburban experience.

2 Schools and Projects Learned About but Not Contacted

Hartford, Connecticut
Proposal: EVERYWHERE SCHOOL
Contact: Jack Dollard, 15 Lewis St., Hartford 06103
Home base: South Arsenal School (a warehouse)
Notes: school to "house" student groups in small spaces throughout the community from which to set out to use available facilities for educational purposes; projects eight multi-instructional areas as home bases for a school program that will be an integral part of community life; each group of 150 students will be served by a master teacher, 4 regular teachers, 5 local paraprofessional aides, 3 teaching associates, and 2 program designers; SAND (South Arsenal Neighborhood Development, Inc.) is currently operating a forerunner to the larger scheme.

Lowell, Massachusetts
Proposal: EDUCATION COMPONENT—LOWELL MODEL CITIES
Contact: Patrick Mogan, Model Cities, 400 Merrimack Street, Lowell 01852
Notes: proposes entire city as potential urban national park to be designated a huge educational complex and human development center; city adapted and furnished with all manner of informational settings related primarily to the industrial heritage of Lowell.

Roxbury, Massachusetts
WAREHOUSE COOPERATIVE SCHOOL
Contact: 100 Magazine St., Roxbury, tel. (617) 427-1112
Data: 81 to 100 students, all ages from 4 on, 8 full-time staff, lots of others.

Sheffield, Massachusetts
STUDY-TRAVEL COMMUNITY SCHOOL
Contact: R.F.D. Box 206, Sheffield, tel. (413) 229-8890
Data: seven students, ages 16 and up
Home base: several, Maine for one
Notes: students travel in relation to projects of their own choosing; built their shelter (yurts) at the Maine base.

Boston, Massachusetts
FLEXIBLE CAMPUS PROGRAM—BOSTON PUBLIC SCHOOLS
Contact: Ken Caldwell, Boston Public Schools, or William Chouinard, Boston Chamber of Commerce
Notes: We know only that it is supposed to involve 12 of Boston's 18 high schools.

Boston, Massachusetts
Project: SIDETRACK
Contact: Carol Kellogg, Boston Public Schools
Notes: Title III ESEA; 7th and 8th grade version of Parkway; 50/50 inner-city and suburban kids; half time regular academic, half time special interest, community electives.

Cambridge/Brookline, Massachusetts
Project: C.I.T.Y. (COMMUNITY INTERACTION THROUGH YOUTH)
Contact: Tom Neel or Ms. Erna Ballantine, 99 Austin St., Cambridge
Notes: Title III ESEA.

New Rochelle, New York
Project: PROGRAM FOR INQUIRY, INVOLVEMENT, AND INDEPENDENT STUDY
Contact: James Gaddy, Principal, 265 Clove St., New Rochelle

Syracuse, New York
SYRACUSE INSTITUTE FOR ENABLING EDUCATION
Contact: 339 E. Onandaga St., Syracuse
Data: private, 18 students, ages 5-12, 5 full-time staff
Notes: utilizing downtown city resources.

Washington, D.C.
FORUM SCHOOL
Contact: 1779 Lanier Place N.W., Washington, tel. (202) 265-5648
Home base: a church
Data: private, 18 students, ages 5-16, 3 full-time staff
Notes: spends much of time traveling around the city.

New Haven, Connecticut
UN-SCHOOL
Contact: Peter Lallos, Educational Services Corp., Box 1126, New Haven, tel. (203) 624-1030, or 562-3690
Data: 24 students, ages 13-18, 5 full-time staff.

Milford, Delaware
Project: THE SEA BESIDE US
Contact: Maura Geens, 906 Lakeview Ave., Milford
Notes: Title III ESEA; grades K-8; open to the entire state; utilizing shore, wetlands, bay, and marine stations.

Annondale-on-Hudson, New York
BARD COLLEGE
Contact: Dr. Reamer Kline, President, Annondale-on-Hudson 12504, tel. (914) 758-6072

Westbury, New York
FRIENDS WORLD COLLEGE
Contact: Ms. Ruth Mary Hill, Vice-President, Mitchel Gardens, Westbury 11590, tel. (516) 224-2616

Plainfield, Vermont
GODDARD COLLEGE
Contact: Dr. Gerald Witherspoon, President, Plainfield 05677, tel. (802) 454-8311

Washington, D.C.
HOWARD UNIVERSITY
Contact: Dr. James Cheek, President, Washington 20001, tel. (202) 636-6040, or Ms. Anita Hackney, UWW Project Director, tel. (202) 636-6792

Amherst, Massachusetts
SCHOOL OF EDUCATION
Contact: Dr. Dwight Allen, Dean, Amherst 01002, tel. (413) 545-0233

Baltimore, Maryland
MORGAN STATE COLLEGE
Contact: Dr. King Cheek, President, Baltimore 21222, tel. (301) 323-2270

Sarasota, Florida
NEW COLLEGE AT SARASOTA
Contact: Dr. John Elmendorf, President, Sarasota 33578, tel. (813) 355-2986

New York, New York
NEW YORK UNIVERSITY
Contact: Dr. Allan Cartter, Chancellor, Washington Square, New York 10003, tel. (212) 598-2323

Bristol, Rhode Island
ROGER WILLIAMS COLLEGE
Contact: Dr. Ralph Gauvey, President, Bristol 02809, tel. (401) 255-2111

Saratoga Springs, New York
SKIDMORE COLLEGE
Contact: Dr. Joseph Palamountain, President, Saratoga Springs 12866, tel. (518) 584-5000

Raleigh, North Carolina
SHAW UNIVERSITY
Contact: Dr. Archie Hargraves, President, Raleigh 27602, tel. (919) 755-4969

Columbia, South Carolina
UNIVERSITY OF SOUTH CAROLINA
Contact: Dr. Thomas Jones, President, Columbia 29208, tel. (803) 777-3101

Staten Island, New York
STATEN ISLAND COMMUNITY COLLEGE
Contact: Dr. William Birenbaum, President, 715 Ocean Terrace, Staten Island 10301, tel. (212) 390-7676

3 Names and Places That Turned Up but Weren't Checked Out

Princeton Junction, Pennsylvania
EREWHON
Bear Brook Rd., tel. (609) 452-2509
Data: private, 53 students, ages 5-18, 9 full-time staff.

Arundel, Maine
THE SCHOOL AROUND US
Data: private, 21 students, ages 4-12, 2 full-time staff.

Poughkeepsie, New York
AMERICAN TRADITION SCHOOL
Box 1025, Poughkeepsie 12601
Data: school without walls for ages 5-17.

New York City
JOAN OF ARC MINI SCHOOL

Needham, Massachusetts
SCHOOL WITHOUT WALLS

Arlington, Maryland
CAMPUS FREE COLLEGE
Box 161, Arlington

Montreal, Quebec, Canada
PARALLEL INSTITUTE
P.O. Box 6, Station D, 104 Quebec

Toronto, Ontario, Canada
LIFE INSTITUTE, EARTHSHIP PROBE, WORLD WILDLIFE EVENT AND EXPANSION OF LOLLIE'S FARM
Contact: Frank Ogden, Ontario College of Art, 100 McCall, tel. (416) 366-4977

New York, New York
TOTAL EDUCATION IN THE TOTAL ENVIRONMENT
Contact: William Eblen or Sherman Price, 50 East 69th, N.Y. 10021, tel. (914) 963-4550 or (212) 744-8700

Osprey, Florida
EKISTIA
Box 368, Osprey, tel. (813) 966-2537
Data: private, 23 students, 3 full-time staff, 3 part-time.

Philadelphia, Pennsylvania
Project: CARE

Mobile, Alabama
EXPERIMENTAL COLLEGE
Contact: University of South Alabama, Mobile 36608

Auburn, Alabama
EXTRACURRICULAR STUDIES PROGRAM
Contact: Union Building—Room 316, Auburn University, Auburn 36830

Storrs, Connecticut
EXPERIMENTAL COLLEGE
Contact: U-8, University of Connecticut, Storrs 06268

New Haven, Connecticut
FREE SCHOOL OF NEW HAVEN
Contact: Dwight Hall, Yale Station, New Haven 06520

Washington, D.C.
NEW UNIVERSITY
Contact: Bob Orser, Suite 605, 1718 P Street NW, Washington 20009

Washington, D.C.
WASHINGTON AREA FREE UNIVERSITY
Contact: 1724 20th Street NW, Washington 20009

Washington, D.C.
GEORGETOWN FREE UNIVERSITY
Contact: P.O. Box 2121, Hoya

Station, Georgetown University, Washington 20007

Newark, Delaware
DELAWARE FREE UNIVERSITY
Contact: University of Delaware, Newark 19711

Tallahassee, Florida
CENTER FOR PARTICIPANT EDUCATION
Contact: 247 University Union, Florida State University, Tallahassee 32306

Atlanta, Georgia
E COLLEGE
tact: Kelly Greene, Emory niversity, Atlanta 30322

nta, Georgia
E UNIVERSITY
act: Student Center, Georgia tute of Technology, Atlan-0332

o, Maine
NAKI EXPERIMENTAL LEGE
tact: 104 Lord Hall, Univer-f Maine, Orono 04473

ma Park, Maryland
E UNIVERSITY
tact: Benjamin L. Henry, tgomery Junior College, ma Park 20012

more, Maryland
NING NETWORKS
act: John Ciekot, 613 n Way, Baltimore 21229

thampton, Massachusetts
TH EXPERIMENTAL LEGE
tact: Jan Kennaugh, 150 Street, Northampton 01060

on, Massachusetts
E UNIVERSITY OF THE LY
tact: 68 St. Stephen St., ton 02115

ton, Massachusetts
ACON HILL FREE SCHOOL
tact: 315 Cambridge Street, ton 02114

ester, Massachusetts
VERSITY
act: Your Place, 806 Main et, Worcester 01610

bridge, Massachusetts
UT FISHING IN AMERICA
tact: 353 Broadway, Cam-ge 02139

ehead, Massachusetts
ERFIELD FREE SCHOOL
ct: 2 Market Square, Mar-ead 01945

over, New Hampshire
RTMOUTH EXPERIMENTAL LLEGE
tact: Hinman Box 493, mouth College, Hanover 55

h Orange, New Jersey
E UNIVERSITY
tact: Seton Hall University, uth Orange 07079

Union, New Jersey
FREE UNIVERSITY
Contact: Student Activities, Newark State College, Union 07083

Rochester, New York
COMMUNIVERSITY
Contact: Genesee Co-op, 942 Monroe Avenue, Rochester 14620

New York, New York
EXPERIMENTAL COLLEGE
Contact: 343 Finley Student Center, City College of New York, 133 St. at Convent Avenue, New York 10031

New York, New York
EMMAUS
Contact: 241 E. 116 Street, New York 10025

New York, New York
FREE LEARNING EXCHANGE
Contact: Paul Knatz, 305 Riverside Drive, Apt. 7E, New York 10025

Clinton, New York
FREE UNIVERSITY
Contact: Kirkland-Hamilton College, Clinton 13323

Syracuse, New York
FREE UNIVERSITY
Contact: Le Moyne College, Le Moyne Heights, Syracuse 13214

Durham, North Carolina
FREE UNIVERSITY
Contact: ASDU, Duke University, Durham 27706

Carrboro, North Carolina
INVISIBLE UNIVERSITY
Contact: King Nyle I, P.O. Box 294, Carrboro 27510

Edinboro, Pennsylvania
FREE UNIVERSITY
Contact: Edinboro State College, P.O. Box 319, Edinboro 16412

Park, Pennsylvania
PENN STATE FREE U
Contact: Hetzl Union Bldg., Park 16802

Philadelphia, Pennsylvania
FREE UNIVERSITY OF PENNSYLVANIA
Contact: COS Office, Houston Hall, 3417 Spruce Street, University of Pennsylvania, Philadelphia 19104

Philadelphia, Pennsylvania
FREE UNIVERSITY
Contact: Box 95, SAC, Temple University, 13th and Montgomery, Philadelphia 19122

Philadelphia, Pennsylvania
FREE UNIVERSITY
Contact: St. Joseph College, Philadelphia 19131

Columbia, South Carolina
SHORT COURSES
Contact: Program Board, University Union, University of South Carolina, Columbia 29208

Fredericksburg, Virginia
FREE UNIVERSITY
Contact: Mary Washington College, Fredericksburg 22401

Charlottesville, Virginia
EXPERIMENTAL UNIVERSITY
Contact: 120 Chancellor Street, Charlottesville 22903

Ontario, Canada
ROCHDALE
Contact: 341 Bloor Street West, Toronto 5, Ontario

Central

1 People, Schools, or Projects Contacted

Chicago, Illinois
METRO SCHOOL
Contact: Nathan Blackman, Principal, 537 South Dearborn St., Chicago 60605

Home base: 537 South Dearborn, 3rd and 4th floors of office building, includes office, lounge, media center, and some classroom space
Data: public, 330 students, grades 9-12
Notes: features "student control over their own learning," which has them outside the school about half the time utilizing the cooperation of some 60 businesses, cultural and civic organizations or institutions through experiences ranging from tours and lectures to in-depth courses.

Cleveland, Ohio
CULC—CLEVELAND URBAN LEARNING COMMUNITY
Contact: Father Tom Shea, Director, c/o St. Ignatius Rectory, W. 30th and Marine, Cleveland
Home base: 2056 East 4th, 5th floor, tel. (216) 523-1875
Data: private, but open; an offshoot of St. Ignatius High, 90 students, ages 16-21, 6 regular staff, lots of educators-at-large
Notes: pursuing Parkway and Metro-like patterns of in-house instruction and community outreach (for example, a pharmacist teaches a chemistry course) at about a one-to-one ratio; features cross-age and peer group tutoring; 1 to 5 suburban-urban ratio and thorough socioeconomic mix.

Golden Valley, Minnesota
Project: COMMUNITY ENVIRONMENTAL STUDIES
Contact: Mike Neylon, Project Director, Minnesota Environmental Science Foundation, 5400 Glenwood, Golden Valley 55422, tel. (612) 544-8971
Data: reaching about 800 5th-12th graders in 30 classes of 25, mostly public, one parochial
Notes: Title III ESEA; variety of small group community study projects; highlight: Students researched, drafted legislation, did some political groundwork on local nonreturnable container ordinance; features cooperative study exchange—inner city/suburban.

New Orleans, Louisiana
GATEWAY SCHOOL
Contact: H.G. Rockenbaugh, 1040 Gov. Nichols Ave., New Orleans
Home base: 1040 Gov. Nichols Ave., tel. (504) 581-2483
Data: public, 150 students, grades 10-12
Notes: so far, patterned quite closely after Parkway and Metro.

Minneapolis, Minnesota
Proposal: MINNESOTA EXPERIMENTAL CITY
Contact: Ron Barnes, tel. (507) 389-6714
Notes: major project for new urban development in which the public education program is being fully considered as a primary form and policy determinant.

2 Schools or Projects Learned About but Not Contacted

St. Louis, Missouri
MATRIX
Contact: Renee Wallace, 1137

81st St., St. Louis, tel. (314) 993-0897

Chicago, Illinois
CAM ACADEMY
Contact: Mary Nelson, 3932 W. Madison Ave., Chicago, tel. (312) 826-6230
Data: private, 250 students, ages 16 and up, 8 full-time staff
Notes: black student body; utilizes school without walls concept; affiliation with University of Illinois Chicago Circle Campus.

Detroit, Michigan
Pilot project: MACKENZIE AND MUMFORD HIGH SCHOOLS
Contact: William Stapp, Dept. of Resources, Planning and Conservation, U. of Michigan, Ann Arbor, Michigan
Notes: 50 lower-income students involved in course work dealing with central-city environmental issues to be followed by discussion encounters with officials and decision makers and culminated by field work related to environmental problems of their choice; hopes to have Detroit schools adopt the project as a regular program feature.

Grand Rapids, Michigan
WALDEN VILLAGE
Contact: Box 114, Grand Rapids 49501, tel. (616) 451-8497
Data: private, accredited by State Board of Education, 38 students, ages 16 and up
Notes: school without walls; planning expansion to two 45-student units.

Wyandotte, Michigan
Project: STRATEGIES FOR ENVIRONMENTAL EDUCATION
Contact: Tom Sparrow, Wyandotte Public Schools, tel. (313) 284-8363
Data: Title III ESEA project involving 30 students in high school, junior high, and elementary school
Notes: cross-age teams investigating local environmental issues and reporting their findings through multimedia presentations.

Yellow Springs, Ohio
ANTIOCH COLLEGE
Contact: Dr. James P. Dixon, President, Yellow Springs 45387
Home base: Antioch College/West, 149 Ninth Street, San Francisco, California, tel. (415) 864-2570

Chicago, Illinois
CHICAGO STATE UNIVERSITY
Contact: Dr. Milton Byrd, President, 6800 So. Stewart, Chicago 60621, tel. (312) 224-3900

Minneapolis, Minnesota
UNIVERSITY OF MINNESOTA
Contact: Dr. Malcolm Moos, President, Minneapolis 55455, tel. (612) 373-2025

Chicago, Illinois
NORTHEASTERN ILLINOIS STATE UNIVERSITY
Contact: Dr. Jerome Sachs, President, Bryn Mawr and St. Louis Avenue, Chicago 60625, tel. (312) 583-4050

Columbia, Missouri
STEPHENS COLLEGE

Contact: Dr. Seymour Smith, President, Columbia 65201, tel. (314) 442-2211

Fulton, Missouri
WESTMINSTER COLLEGE
Contact: Dr. Robert L.D. Davidson, President, Fulton 65251

3 Names and Places That Turned Up but Weren't Checked Out

Ann Arbor, Michigan
PIONEER II
Contact: Bill Casello, Ann Arbor Public Schools
Notes: school without walls prototype, 100 students, grades 9-12.

Ann Arbor, Michigan
Proposal: COMMUNITY HIGH
Contact: Dean Bodley, Ann Arbor Public Schools

New Orleans, Louisiana
ALTERNATIVE HIGH SCHOOL
Contact: Frank and Betty Cole, 7919 Oak, New Orleans
Data: 50 students, 80 resource people
Notes: involved in a voucher system challenge to Lousiana school laws.

Milwaukee, Wisconsin
SCHOOL WITHOUT WALLS

Minneapolis, Minnesota
Project: SOUTHEAST ALTERNATIVES
Notes: one of HEW-U.S. Office of Education Experimental Schools projects, which features comprehensive K-12 innovation strategies.

Tucson, Arizona
FREE UNIVERSITY
Contact: University of Arizona, Tucson 85721

Fayetteville, Arkansas
THE FREE UNIVERSITY
Contact: P.O. Box 1608, Fayetteville 72701

State College, Mississippi
FREE UNIVERSITY
Contact: YMCA, Mississippi State University, State College 39762

Kansas City, Missouri
COMMUNIVERSITY
Contact: UMKC-5100 Rockhill Road, Kansas City 64110

Lincoln, Nebraska
NEBRASKA FREE UNIVERSITY
Contact: Nebraska Union 331, University of Nebraska, Lincoln 68508

East Lansing, Michigan
MICHIGAN STATE PERVERSITY
Contact: U.N. Lounge, Union Building, Michigan State University, East Lansing 48823

Kalamazoo, Michigan
FREE UNIVERSITY
Contact: Kalamazoo College, Kalamazoo 49001

Ann Arbor, Michigan
FREE UNIVERSITY OF ANN ARBOR
Contact: U.A.C., Michigan Union, Ann Arbor 48104

Detroit, Michigan
FREE UNIVERSITY
Contact: Box 142 University Center, Room 309, Wayne State University, Detroit 48202

Detroit, Michigan
FREE COMMUNITY SCHOOL
Contact: Project Headline, 13267 Gratiot, Detroit 48205

Minneapolis, Minnesota
MINNESOTA FREE UNIVERSITY
Contact: 1417 First Avenue South, No. 210, Minneapolis 55403

Minneapolis, Minnesota
JUDSON LIFE SCHOOL
Contact: 4101 Harriet Ave. So., Minneapolis 55409

Northfield, Minnesota
FREE UNIVERSITY
Contact: St. Olaf College, Northfield 55057

Chicago, Illinois
ALTERNATE UNIVERSITY
Contact: Box 4348, Room 317, University of Illinois, Chicago Circle Campus, Chicago 60680

Evanston, Illinois
EVANSTON LEARNING EXCHANGE
Contact: 828 Davis Street, Evanston 60201

DeKalb, Illinois
LIVING/LEARNING
Contact: Northern Illinois University, DeKalb 60115

Edwardsville, Illinois
SWILC—Southwestern Illinois Learning Coop.
Contact: Community Involvement Project, Student Activities, Southern Illinois University, Edwardsville 62025

Indianapolis, Indiana
FREE UNIVERSITY
Contact: Bethlehem Lutheran Church, 526 E. 52nd Street, Indianapolis 46205

Muncie, Indiana
FREE UNIVERSITY OF MUNCIE
Contact: Student Center-B3, Ball State University, Muncie 47306

Bloomington, Indiana
FREE UNIVERSITY
Contact: Union Board Office, Indiana Memorial Union, Bloomington 47401

Lawrence, Kansas
KANSAS FREE UNIVERSITY
Contact: Student Activity Center, 1314 Oread, Lawrence 66044

Manhattan, Kansas
UNIVERSITY FOR MAN
Contact: 615 Fairchild Terrace, Manhattan 66502

Lexington, Kentucky
FREE UNIVERSITY
Contact: Student Government, University of Kentucky, Lexington 40506

Louisville, Kentucky
FREE UNIVERSITY
Contact: Student Government, University of Louisville, Louisville 40208

Baton Rouge, Louisiana
FREE UNIVERSITY
Contact: Student Activities Offices, LSU Union, Louisiana State University, Baton Rouge 70803

New Orleans, Louisiana
FREE UNIVERSITY OF NEW ORLEANS
Contact: 1232 St. Mary, New Orleans 70130

Albuquerque, New Mexico
AMISTAD
Contact: Room 1060, Mesa Visa, University of New Mexico, Albuquerque 87106

Bowling Green, Ohio
NEW UNIVERSITY
Contact: Bowling Green State University, Bowling Green 43402

University Heights, Ohio
FREE UNIVERSITY
Contact: John Carroll University, University Heights 44118

Delaware, Ohio
FREE UNIVERSITY
Contact: Student Activities, Ohio Wesleyan University, Delaware 43015

Tulsa, Oklahoma
FREE UNIVERSITY
Contact: Canterbury Center, 2839 E. 5th, Tulsa 74104

Knoxville, Tennessee
FREE UNIVERSITY
Contact: Student Senate Office, University of Tennessee, Knoxville 37916

Nashville, Tennessee
FREE UNIVERSITY NASHVILLE
Contact: Gregg Thomas, Box 2975, Station B, Vanderbilt University, 21st Ave. and West End, Nashville 37203

Dallas, Texas
FREE UNIVERSITY
Contact: 214 Student Center, Southern Methodist University, Dallas 75222

Arlington, Texas
FREE UNIVERSITY
Contact: Student Congress, University of Texas, Arlington 76010

Waco, Texas
FREE UNIVERSITY
Contact: Student Government Office, Baylor University, Waco 76703

Houston, Texas
UNIVERSITY OF THOUGHT
Contact: 3505 S. Main, Houston 77002

El Paso, Texas
FREE UNIVERSITY
Contact: Oscar Wright, 1219 N. Oregon, Apt. 9, El Paso 79902

San Antonio, Texas
UNIVERSIDAD DE LOS BARRIOS
Contact: 1220 Buena Vista, San Antonio 78207

West

1 People, Schools, or Projects Contacted

Seattle, Washington
NOVA SCHOOL
Contact: Dave Powell, c/o Nova YWCA, 5th and Seneca, Seattle, tel. (206) 587-5072
Home base: YWCA, 5th and Seneca
Data: public, 90 students, grades 10-12
Notes: school without walls program that meets regular grad-

uation requirements through alternative forms; 50 percent of classes conducted by community educators-at-large; mobility due to free public transportation throughout the city; university course auditing; school mime troup is key part of presentation advocating and explaining "alternative" education.

Seattle/Tacoma, Washington
Project: QUALITY OF LIFE
Contact: Puget Sound Coali[tion?], Marvin Durnig, 1411 4th Av[e], Seattle, tel. (206) 624-8901
Notes: community-neighbor[hood] network of 400 discussion/a[ction?] groups, which base their lea[rn]ing experience on shared imp[res]sions of a series of eight the[matic?] television presentations with[in] related readings and simple i[n]formation gathering tasks; m[?] award-winning project in 19[?]

San Francisco, California
WHEELS
Contact: William Edison, Wh[eel]master, 280 Divisadero St., S[an] Francisco, tel. (415) 863-55[?]
Home base: Edison's attic, w[hen] necessary; otherwise, a Dodg[e] van
Data: private ($800/year), 9[?] students, ages 9-14, 2 teache[rs]
Notes: program centers on d[?] covering problems, defining [?] and tracing them around the [?] to seek alternative solutions; for instance, conflicting "ex[pert?] testimony" about bay water pollution prompted student[s] to gather data of their own; program includes camping e[x]perience, related back to urb[an] circumstance.

Daly City, California
JEFFERSON WILDERNESS SCHOOL
Contact: Bill Curran, 6996 Mission St., Daly City
Data: public school, 25 stud[ents] per semester, grades 10-12
Notes: program begins with [a] two-week wilderness trip to [?] build human community and [?] then features (1) urban proj[ect?] (2) work on model environm[en]tal developments on Nature [Con]servancy lands striving for 9[0] percent resource recycling, a[nd] (3) the Truck Farm organic gardening; activity takes plac[e] in project teams of 2 to 10 p[ar]ticipants each.

American Fork, Utah
Project: OUTDOOR CURRIC[U]LUM FOR ALL SEASONS
Contact: Lyle Tregaskis, 50 [?] No. Center, American Fork, tel. (801) 756-3579
Data: reaches 18,000 stude[nts?] Alpine school district, grade[s] 1-12 with elementary emph[asis]
Notes: utilizing local enviro[n]ment in ongoing curriculum through experiences available within local county boundarie[s] two major aspects: schoolgrou[nd] and neighborhood utilization and field experience requiring transportation; study of landscape, architecture, water use, population density, plants, animals, and urbanization pressure; card system featuring suggestions for teachers, accounts of student experiences; 9th graders training as guides for younger people.

Portland, Oregon
QUINCY SCHOOL
Contact: Jerry Conrath, Director, Portland School District No. 1
Home base: John Adams High School
Data: public, 125 students, grades 9-12
Notes: school within a school, emphasizing two-way community access and featuring three interdependent learning "structures": personal counseling and developme[nt], career options, and the "urb[an] classroom."

Los [Ang]eles, California
MO[...]
Co[ntact]: Charles Rusch, School of [Archit]ecture and Urban Planning, [UC]LA
Da[ta]: [pri]vate, 7 students, ages 9-1[...]
No[tes]: converted Ford van; sta[rted] with local publication, "W[hat t]o Do with Your Kids in [...]; uses city libraries in m[eetin]gs for basic skills and res[earch] work; much activity cen[ters o]n investigation of city sys[tems] (for example, legal—en[force]ment, administration of jus[tice a]nd legislative process—or [distr]ibution—food, power, ser[vices,] etc.); makes nature inv[estig]ation trips—ocean, desert, m[ounta]in.

Co[rvalli]s, Oregon
Pr[oject:] **WORLD OF WORK**
Co[ntact]: Thomas Hornig, 4512 Jo[...] [R]oad, Corvallis
No[tes]: Title III ESEA project—Oc[cupa]tional Exploratory Program [fo]r a Modern Junior High—to [pr]ovide experiences that can [...] be incorporated into reg[ular] school curriculum with im[medi]ate objective of bridging th[e gap] between the background inf[orm]ation of junior high and the re[aliti]es of post-high-school em[ploy]ment; "community class-ro[om]—not job training but ob[serva]tion, questioning, and as[sistan]ce related to some 40 "s[kill]s" in the community.

De[nver,] Colorado
Pr[oject]: **BALARAT CENTER FO[R E]NVIRONMENTAL ST[UDI]ES**
C[ontac]t: Kenneth Horn, Denver Pu[blic] Schools
N[otes]: comprehensive K-12 e[nviron]mental education pro[gram in]cludes one-day field [experien]ces, urban environment stu[dy, K-]6, outdoor leadership [tra]ining for youth, career education programs, one-week ou[tdoor] resident school, and m[axim]um use of the Denver environment; program features use [of a] 750-acre wilderness site 47 [mile]s northwest of Denver

Berkeley, California
BERKELEY ALTERNATIVE SCHOOLS PROGRAM
Contact: Larry Wells, Program Coordinator, Berkeley Public Schools
Data: total of 18 public mini-schools, 17 more being planned for fall 1972, 1200 students in the 6 high school alternatives
Notes: now under federal Experimental Schools funding; program is entire complex of voluntary alternative schools within the Berkeley system attempting to administer to the obvious diversity of needs, interests, and learning styles within a large multiracial public school population; little programmatic emphasis (in the Parkway sense) on urban experiences, but the particular significance of this program is not in any exemplary or explicit use of the city as a learning resource so much as in the tremendous potential inherent in such a major system-wide effort to meet special needs and capitalize on special opportunities—so that the people, places, and processes of the city will naturally be more apparent as vital resources, and educational concerns will be more recognizable as valid urban form determinants.

2 Schools or Projects Learned About but Not Contacted

San Francisco, California
ATHENIAN SCHOOL URBAN CENTER
Contact: Terry Diehl, 149 9th St., San Francisco
Home base: a house on Sacramento St.
Data: private, 40 students, high school
Notes: provides urban-centered study and experience for the Athenian School, Danville, California; students in various "internship" positions.

San Francisco, California
URBAN SCHOOL OF SAN FRANCISCO
Contact: 2938 Washington St., San Francisco 94115, tel. (415) 922-5552
Data: private, 90 students, ages 13 and up, 16 full-time staff
Notes: accredited school; has been using the city as a classroom since at least 1966.

Berkeley, California
SAFARI SCHOOL
Contact: 1310 Acton # C, Berkeley, tel. (415) 527-7069
Data: private, 30 students, ages 11-15, 3 full-time staff
Notes: goal is to "make expeditions to every conceivable place within 100-mile radius" and learn through seminars, labs, research, tutorials, and individual projects.

San Francisco, California
ON LOCATION
Contact: Duncan McSwain, Redwood High School, Larkspur, California
Notes: urban experience and internships for students of a "suburban" Bay Area public school.

San Francisco, California
SYMBAS
Contact: Rich Burkhardt, 1380 Howard St., San Francisco 94103, tel. (410) 863-3787
Home base: a generous ground floor space in Project One, a warehouse adapted to house a complex of more or less counterculture creative endeavors.
Data: private ($100-500/year), 35 students, ages 13-18, 3 full-time, 5 part-time staff, and the rest of Project One.

Santa Cruz, California
SANTA CRUZ COMMUNITY SCHOOL
Contact: 461 Redwood Dr., Santa Cruz 95060, tel. (415) 426-9991
Data: private, 100 students, ages 4 and up, full-time staff of 13
Notes: uses community as resource; operates in groups of 15 to 20; associated with University of California at Santa Cruz.

Walnut Creek, California
RURBAN
Contact: 55 Eckley Lane, Walnut Creek 94598, tel. (415) 939-1766
Data: private ($500/year), 25 students, ages 13 and up, 5 full-time staff, 15 part-time, gives scholarships.

San Francisco, California
MERCY HIGH URBAN EXPERIENCE
Contact: Sister Mary Gabriel Nelson
Data: parochial, 40 seniors
Notes: 2-semester urban experience.

San Francisco, California
LONE MOUNTAIN COLLEGE URBAN EXPERIENCE
Contact: Sue Robinson, Coro Foundation, 149 9th St., San Francisco 94103, tel. (415) 863-4601
Data: 40 undergraduates
Notes: provides public affairs and public service internships and training; the Coro Foundation has been involved in similar efforts since 1947.

Berkeley, California
PEOPLE'S COMMUNITY SCHOOL
Contact: Box 4133, Berkeley 94704, tel. (415) 841-4769
Data: private (scholarships), 35 students, ages 4-12, 3 full-time staff, 21 part-time
Notes: school without walls with extensive parental involvement, which includes teaching.

Long Beach, California
NEW DIRECTIONS
Contact: Beverly Mitchell, P.O. Box 2881, Long Beach, tel. (213) 597-8320 or (213) 434-3997
Data: private (scholarships), 23 students, 4 full-time staff
Notes: meets in the park.

Eugene, Oregon
EDUCATIONAL ENVIRONMENTS
Contact: Bill Shephard (parent and founder), Psychology Dept., University of Oregon, tel. (503) 686-4904 or 896-3885
Notes: started as preschool, expands by adding new preschoolers each year; thesis is concentration of instruction that then enables wide-ranging firsthand exploration in two basic ways: (1) intense 20-minute sessions of basic skills instruction at 1 to 8 teacher-student ratio frees at least half the day for community outreach; (2) they intend to provide the equivalent of high school education by seventh grade age and then "turn kids loose" in the world for the "extra" years.

Yellow Springs, Ohio
ANTIOCH COLLEGE
Contact: Dr. James P. Dixon, President, Yellow Springs 45387

Home base: Antioch College/West, 149 Ninth Street, San Francisco, California 94103, tel. (415) 864-2570

Denver, Colorado
LORETTO HEIGHTS COLLEGE
Contact: Sister Patricia Jean Manion, President, 3001 So. Federal Blvd., Denver 80326, tel. (303) 922-4011

3 Names and Places That Turned Up but Weren't Checked Out

Van Nuys, California
SHERWOOD OAKS HIGH/ JR. HIGH
Contact: 6725 Valjean (or 6730 Vesper), Van Nuys 91406, tel. (213) 781-9360
Data: private ($200-$1200/year), 25 students, ages 13-16, 7 full-time staff
Notes: travel a lot, founded in 1948, went experimental in 1967; associated with an experimental college.

Venice, California
PERIPATETIC
Contact: 1327 Toms Blvd. Venice, tel. (213) 399-8160

Seattle, Washington
EARTH STATION SEVEN
Contact: 402 15th Ave., Seattle 98112, tel. (206) EA 9-8300

Neah Bay, Washington
Project: **NEAH BAY COMMUNITY STUDIES**
Contact: Warren Adams, Northwest Regional Education Laboratory, Portland, Oregon
Notes: junior high students in comprehensive study of and service to a small community.

Arcata, California
ARCATA FREE UNIVERSITY
Contact: 1628 G Street, Arcata 95521

Pomona, California
EXPERIMENTAL COLLEGE
Contact: California Polytechnic Institute, Pomona 91766

Los Angeles, California
EXPERIMENTAL COLLEGE
Contact: California State College, Student Activities Office, Administration 123, 5151 State College Drive, Los Angeles 90037

Long Beach, California
EXPERIMENTAL COLLEGE
Contact: Associated Students Office, California State College, 6101 E. 7th, Long Beach 90801

Sacramento, California
ALTERNATIVE EDUCATION
Contact: ASSSC, Sacramento State College, Sacramento 95819

San Diego, California
EXPERIMENTAL COLLEGE
Contact: Organizations Center, Aztec Center, San Diego State College, San Diego 92115

Northridge, California
EXPERIMENTAL COLLEGE
Contact: San Fernando Valley State College, 9520 Etiwanda, Northridge 91324

San Jose, California
EXPERIMENTAL COLLEGE
Contact: San Jose State College, College Union Building, Laguna Seca Room 211, South 9th Street, San Jose 95112

San Francisco, California
EXPERIMENTAL COLLEGE
Contact: City College of San
Francisco, 50 Phelan Avenue,
San Francisco 94112

San Francisco, California
ENTROPY
Contact: 1914 Polk, San Fran-
cisco 94109

San Anselmo, California
FAMILY MIX
Contact: 43 Mariposa, San Ansel-
mo 94960

Berkeley, California

FREE UNIVERSITY OF
BERKELEY
Contact: 2000 Parker Street,
Berkeley 94704

Solana Beach, California
FREE UNIVERSITY OF SAN
DIEGO
Contact: 703 N. Rios Avenue,
Solana Beach 92075

San Francisco, California
HELIOTROPE
Contact: 21 Columbus, San
Francisco 94111

San Francisco, California
ORPHEUS
Contact: 1385 7th Avenue,
San Francisco 94122

San Jose, California
SAN JOSE FREE UNIVERSITY
Contact: 50 S. 4th, No. 3, San
Jose 95113

Van Nuys, California
SHERWOOD OAKS EXP.
COLLEGE
Contact: 6725 Valjean Avenue,
Van Nuys 91406

Los Angeles, California
EXPERIMENTAL COLLEGE
Contact: Associated Students,
Student Union 321, University
of Southern California, Los
Angeles 90007

Davis, California
EXPERIMENTAL COLLEGE
Contact: A.S.U.C.D., University
of California, Davis 95616

Irvine, California
EXPERIMENTAL COLLEGE
Contact: Associated Students
Office, University of California,
Irvine 92664

Los Angeles, California
EXPERIMENTAL COLLEGE
Contact: 407 Kirkhov Hall,
University of California, Los
Angeles 90024

Monterey, California
UNIVERSITY FOR MAN
Contact: Room 5A, Monterey
Peninsula College, 980 Fremont
Extension, Monterey 93940

Boulder, Colorado
COMMUNITY FREE SCHOOL
Contact: 1030 13th Street,
Boulder 80302

Greeley, Colorado
FREE UNIVERSITY OF
COLORADO STATE
Contact: Box 12-Fraiser, Colorado
State College, Greeley 80631

Denver, Colorado
DENVER FREE UNIVERSITY
Contact: 1122 E. 17th Avenue,
Denver 80218

Eugene, Oregon
SEARCH
Contact: 305 Erb Memorial
Union, Eugene 97403

Portland, Oregon
FREE UNIVERSITY
Contact: Student Activities,
Lewis and Clark College, Port-
land 97219

Salt Lake City, Utah
FREE UNIVERSITY OF UTAH
Contact: Student Activities
Center, University of Utah,
Salt Lake City 84112

Bellingham, Washington
NORTHWEST FREE UNIVER-
SITY
Contact: P.O. Box 1255, Belling-
ham 98225

Milwaukee, Wisconsin
FREE UNIVERSITY
Contact: Associated Students,
620 N. 14th Street, Milwaukee
53233

Madison, Wisconsin
FREE UNIVERSITY
Contact: Henry D. Keesing, P.O.
Box 965, Madison 53701

Alberta, Canada
FREE UNIVERSITY NORTH
c/o S.C.M.
Contact: Box 106, University
of Alberta, Edmonton, Alberta

British Columbia, Canada
VANCOUVER FREE UNIVER-
SITY
Contact: 1895 Venables Street,
Vancouver, British Columbia

As we said, this list is by no means
comprehensive, but we are anxious
to expand and update it for later
editions of the *Yellow Pages of
Learning Resources.* If we missed
any program that you are involved
in or that you know about, please
let us know the details.

Richard Saul Wurman
GEE!
1214 Arch Street
Philadelphia, Pennsylvania 19107

Peter Way Cotton
Alternative Schools Program
U Mass School of Education
Amherst, Massachusetts 01002

94

Yellow Pages of Learning Resources
edited by Richard Saul Wurman

"The city is education," this book proclaims. "The city is education—and the architecture of education rarely has much to do with the building of schools. The city is a schoolhouse, and its ground floor is both bulletin board and library. The graffiti of the city are its window displays announcing events; they should reveal its people to themselves, tell about what they're doing and why and where they're doing it. Everything we do—if described, made clear, and made observable—is education: the 'Show and Tell,' the city itself.... It is a classroom without walls, an open university for people of all ages offering a boundless curriculum with unlimited expertise. If we can make our urban environment comprehensible and observable, we will have created classrooms with endless windows on the world."

The design of this book imitates the Yellow Pages telephone directory, but the intent is not to "let your fingers do the walking"—the book is meant to draw you out into the environment, to put you in contact with a lot of different kinds of people, to teach you the what, where, why, and how-to of all sorts of things that go on in the real world. The intent, finally, is to let your head do the thinking, your eyes do the seeing, and—it's good exercise—your feet do the walking. "...The city is everywhere around us, and it is rife with invaluable learning resources. Even more than classrooms and teachers, the most valuable learning resources in the city are the people, places, and processes that we encounter every day. But in order to realize the vast learning potential of these resources, we must learn to learn from them."

Yellow Pages of Learning Resources is a guide to the city—any city, any town. It consists of some seventy alphabetically arranged categories and tells how to tune them in and why they are important to know about. It is a specific guide to people (the pharmacist, the taxi-cab driver), to places (the airport, the courtroom), and to processes (candy making, city planning). Here are some others: architect—bricklayer—cemetery—dry cleaner—electrician—food distribution center—garbage man—hospital—insurance company—junk yard—kindergarten room—locksmith—museum—next-door neighbor—orchestra member—paper box factory—quarry—real estate broker—social worker—tree stump (tree stump?)—union boss—vacant lot—weather forecasting—x-ray technician—Yellow Pages telephone directory—zoo.

Other possibilities are left to the imagination of students and teachers; these resources can then be sought out once the book has made it clear how to get around. "Student" here can be anybody—while the book is within the range of school-age children, it is also open to adults, except those who already know how locks work, who the next-door neighbor is, and what ward leaders *really* do. They are excused from class and are free to go out and learn something new on the way home or *at* home (like, why doesn't the furnace thermostat work?). Some of the resources listed are also especially suitable for group learning experiences, and thus the book becomes a valuable tool for the teacher, parent, boy or girl scout leader, or adult education leader.

Richard Saul Wurman is a partner in the architecture and planning firm of Murphy Levy Wurman in Philadelphia. His interest in education prompted the formation of GEE!, Group for Environmental Education Inc., which developed *Our Man-Made Environment—Book Seven;* his interest in urban graphics is displayed in *Urban Atlas: 20 American Cities, Making the City Observable,* and *Man-Made Philadelphia.* All these publications are available from The MIT Press.

The MIT Press
Massachusetts Institute of Technology
Cambridge, Massachusetts 02142

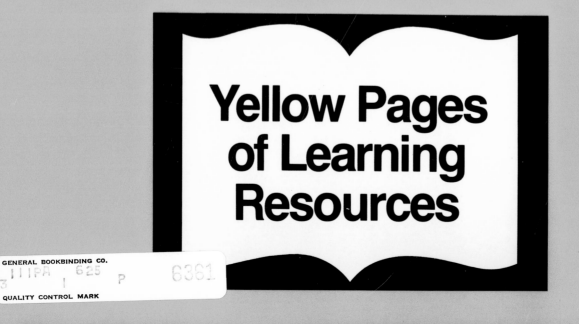

Yellow Pages
of Learning
Resources

WYF

DATE DUE